Paper
Celebrations

Jane Alford

D&C
David and Charles

A DAVID & CHARLES BOOK
Copyright © David & Charles Limited 2008

David & Charles is an F+W Publications Inc. company
4700 East Galbraith Road, Cincinnati, OH 45236

Text and designs copyright © Jane Alford 2008
Photography copyright © David & Charles 2008

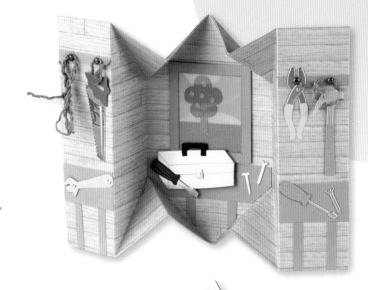

A catalogue record for this book is available from the
British Library.

ISBN-13: 978-0-7153-2793-7 hardback
ISBN-10: 0-7153-2793-3 hardback

ISBN-13: 978-0-7153-2781-4 paperback
ISBN-10: 0-7153-2781-X paperback

Printed in China by SNP Leefung Pte Ltd
for David & Charles
Brunel House   Newton Abbot   Devon

Senior Commissioning Editor Cheryl Brown
Desk Editor Bethany Dymond
Senior Designer Charly Bailey
Designer Eleanor Stafford
Production Controller Ros Napper
Project Editor Betsy Hosegood
Photographer Karl Adamson and Kim Sayer

Visit our website at www.davidandcharles.co.uk

David & Charles books are available from all good bookshops;
alternatively you can contact our Orderline on 0870 9908222 or
write to us at FREEPOST EX2 110, D&C Direct, Newton Abbot,
TQ12 4ZZ (no stamp required UK only); US customers call
800-289-0963 and Canadian customers call 800-840-5220.

Contents

Introduction

This book was created with important celebrations in mind because it is at these times that you want to give something that stands out from the ordinary. You might require an extra-special card or want something a bit different such as a mini album, a wall hanging, gift basket or presentation box. You'll find them all here.

The main part of the book is divided into 12 chapters, each based on a particular technique and with a special occasion in mind. But every chapter also includes some alternative designs for other occasions, so no matter what event you are thinking of, you'll find plenty of different ideas.

The first technique is a delightfully novel idea to celebrate a new baby – a stunning **concertina book with pockets** to hold tags with special messages (see page 12). And if there isn't a baby about, what about a Christmas-tree decoration, as shown below right, or wedding invitation card?

If you like the idea of having several pages and pockets for messages, take a look at the Valentine card on page 52, where **heart-shaped pages** are embellished with pockets and mini cards. There are also three more versions of this card, with teddy, tulip and butterfly pages suitable for many other occasions, or you could adapt the idea to design your own cards.

If **shaped cards** are what most appeal to you, you'll love the two delightful house cards in the Wonder Folds chapter on page 20. The first card has double doors that open to reveal the welcoming interior and an alternative version has a garden scene with a thatched cottage in the distance. You'll also find ideas here for adapting these cards for a Nativity scene or a card just for men.

You'll also like the shaped **cut-out cards** on pages 94–99, which feature a versatile handbag card that will be popular with women and girls, with clever fan, gift and wedding-cake shapes too.

Other lovely cards for you to make include the pretty daffodil Easter card on page 86 (shown in the centre opposite), which features a clever

pricked and painted design, along with some other ideas for using pricking to make scented sachets and Christmas decorations. Or try the lovely fan card and its matching gift box (bottom right and pages 66–70), which are made using **teabag folding** techniques.

If you want to make a gift too, take a look at the silver wedding album on page 36. This is just an ordinary **photo album** that has been re-covered and then decorated on the front with an iris-folded design. You can use this idea to spruce up any album or even a box or gift bag (see pages 40–41). There's a mini album on page 80 if you would prefer something smaller, or you might like to make a **hanging** like the one on page 72, designed for a 21st birthday celebration. This can be adapted to make a gorgeous **christening book**.

Whether you are making your own gift or purchasing one, you'll want to present it as beautifully as possible, and although you can wrap it, a box like the one shown top right (see page 78) becomes part of the gift itself and can be kept forever. For Christmas, there's a trio of mini **shaped boxes** (page 30) that can be filled with sweets, biscuits or small toys and hung from the tree. You can also make larger versions for those awkwardly shaped presents or use them for other occasions (see page 35).

The daffodil Easter card is accompanied by its own matching **gift bag**, (see page 90), while the fan card comes with a gift box (see right and page 66) or you could make a gift bag especially for a man (see page 41). For Halloween, make pumpkin, witch or bat **baskets** to fill with treats. These can also be adapted for other occasions – see the Chinese lanterns, confetti cone and Easter basket on pages 64–65.

If you find you need any extra help making the projects here, refer to the information at the front of the book, which includes instructions on folding paper or card, making tassels and covering albums and boxes. If you are a seasoned crafter you may not need to look at this section, but it is there in case you want a refresher.

I hope that making the projects in this book gives you many hours of pleasure and that the ideas here fire your imagination to come up with your own projects.

Happy crafting.

Jane Alford

Tools & Techniques

This chapter covers the basic tools and techniques required for the projects in this book – any specific techniques required to make a particular project are explained in full in the step-by-step instructions. Here you'll find out how to choose the right paper or card, how to cover an album or a box and how to make a tassel as a finishing touch.

Basic Tool Kit

Before embarking on paper-crafting techniques there are a few tools and materials you'll need to collect. This tool kit contains the basics.

Adhesives

Glue stick to glue paper to paper.

PVA glue or glue pen to attach beads, sequins or buttons.

Double-sided tape to glue large pieces of paper or card together (or use glue stick).

Spray adhesive when you want a strong, smooth bond, as when covering an album.

Low-tack tape to secure a tracing over your paper or other item temporarily.

Sticky foam pads to attach shapes and raise them off the surface.

Cutting tools

Sharp, pointed scissors for intricate cutting.

General-purpose scissors for cutting big shapes (keep a pair exclusively for cutting paper or card).

Craft knife with a sharp blade for removing small areas or cutting straight lines.

Cutting mat for use with a craft knife.

Metal ruler to aid cutting straight lines with a knife.

Guillotine for fast, accurate cutting (optional).

Scoring and folding

Metal ruler for drawing straight lines, cutting or scoring against.

Bone folder for creasing folds neatly.

Handling tools

Tweezers for holding tiny punched shapes, sequins and so on.

Cocktail sticks for applying tiny amounts of glue.

Marking and measuring tools

HB pencil for drawing templates and cutting lines and a **2B pencil** for marks that will be erased later.

Soft eraser for removing pencil marks.

Ruler or tape measure for accurate measuring.

Brushes and pens

Watercolour brushes for applying watercolour or acrylic paint.

Glue brush for applying glue accurately (keep a separate brush for this purpose because it ruins the brush).

Outliners for adding details.

Coloured pens and markers for adding greetings and detailing.

Punching and pricking tools

Pricking tool in fine and medium or thick sizes.

Pricking mat, which is softer than a cutting mat – or use a piece of dense foam, such as a mouse mat.

Eyelet punch for fitting eyelets, making holes for brads or making decorative holes.

Hole punch for punching holes in tags.

Bradawl or other perforating tool for making holes for brads.

Choosing and Using Card

The ideal thickness of your card will depend on what it is to be used for in your project. 160–180gsm card is ideal for folded projects, 200–230gsm for projects requiring medium-weight card and 280–300gsm for projects requiring heavy-weight card. To fold the card neatly, refer to these instructions.

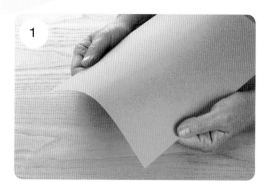

Find the grain of your card by gently folding the card widthways and then lengthways. Whichever bends the easiest is the direction of the grain. Try to fold with the grain where possible for the neatest results.

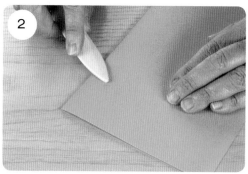

Use a pencil to mark the folding lines. Score along the lines by running a bone folder or the back of a scissor or knife blade along a ruler's edge. Fold the card along the scored lines and press the fold with a bone folder to create a sharp crease.

Covering an Album

You can buy plain notebooks, albums and drawing books from most stationery shops, but often the cover doesn't suit your purpose. Luckily it is easy to add your own cover following these simple instructions.

Right card, right job

Use thin card for decorative shapes, medium-weight card for greetings cards and thick card for gift boxes.

Cut a piece of paper the size of the book or album plus 2.5cm (1in) all round. Lay the paper wrong side up and spray with adhesive. Open the book and press it centrally on top. Cut a small triangle on each side of the spine at the top and bottom and another across each of the corners just a small distance away from the book.

Fold and glue the edges of the paper over to the inside and push the paper at the top and bottom of the spine inside it. Cut two pieces of thin card slightly smaller than the inside covers of the album and stick these in place using double-sided tape.

You will need

Album or book

Paper to cover the album

Thin white card (or a coordinating colour)

Spray adhesive

Double-sided tape

Scissors

Tape measure or ruler

Making a Tassel

Tassels are attractive finishing details that will enhance many paper projects. They are only available in the shops in limited colours, but it is easy to make one yourself and that way you can ensure that you get just the colour and size you need.

You will need

Card rectangle the size of the required tassel

Embroidery cotton (floss)

Scissors

The tassel on the bottom of this fan provides added body and movement. By making the tassel yourself, you can be sure that it is just right for your project. See page 98 to make this Mother's Day card.

1

Cut a piece of card the required size of the tassel and wind it with embroidery cotton (floss) until the tassel is the desired thickness.

2

Tie the loops tightly along one edge of the card with another length of thread and slip off the card.

Two tone

You don't have to use just one colour of cotton (floss) to make a tassel. Two toning colours work well together or you could use a multi-coloured embroidery cotton.

3

Use another length of embroidery cotton (floss) to bind the top, concealing the ends in the main body of the tassel. Trim the loops at the bottom of the tassel.

Covering a Box

Presenting a gift, card or album in a box always makes it look more important and valuable. You can make your own boxes (see page 30, for example), buy plain boxes or recycle old ones, but you'll want to cover them to coordinate with your card and tag. Here are some simple instructions for covering square or rectangular boxes.

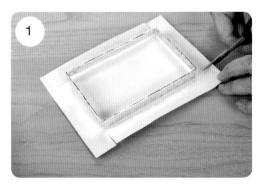

Cut a piece of paper large enough to cover the lid and sides plus 2cm (¾in) all round. Lay out the paper wrong side up and glue the lid right side down in the centre. Make a cut to each corner of the lid, as shown.

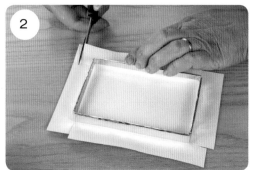

Trim the four overlaps at the corners slightly by cutting off a small section, as shown.

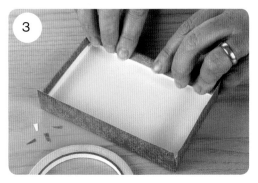

Stick the paper to the sides of the lid using double-sided tape, tucking the flaps under the side pieces. At each corner, cut a slim triangle in the excess paper down to the edge of the lid. Fold the paper over and glue it to the inside of the lid edge.

This little box is used to store a pretty Christening book. The paper covering matches the papers used for the book for perfect coordination. See page 78 for this project.

Cut a piece of paper to fit around the box with a small overlap and 4cm (1½in) deeper. Stick the paper to the box with double-sided tape, leaving a 2cm (¾in) overlap at the top and bottom. Make cuts at the top and bottom corners as in step 1 and fold and glue the paper along the top edge to the inside of the box. Glue the long sides of the paper to the bottom of the box, trim the short sides diagonally and then glue these over the long sides. If desired, cover the bottom of the box with a rectangle of paper cut to fit, sticking it in place with double-sided tape.

Perfect papers

Papers with small patterns are easiest to use for covering boxes, or use geometric designs such as stripes or checks.

You will need

Square or rectangular box with lid

Two sheets of paper, one for the box and another for the lid

Double-sided tape

Glue stick

Scissors

Tape measure or ruler

Covering a Round Box

It may seem more of a challenge to cover a round box than a square or rectangular one, but with the help of some double-sided tape it is really quite straightforward.

You will need

- Square or rectangular box with lid
- Two sheets of paper, one for the box and another for the lid
- Double-sided tape
- Glue stick
- Scissors
- Tape measure or ruler

Cut a circle of paper, 2.5cm (1in) larger in diameter than the lid. Lay it out right side down and glue the lid face down in the centre. Snip around the edge of the circle at 6mm (¼in) intervals and stick the tabs to the edge of the lid using short strips of double-sided tape. Cut another strip of paper 1.5cm (⅝in) bigger than the depth of the lid and long enough to fit round it with a 1cm (⅜in) overlap.

Use double-sided tape to stick the strip to the edge of the lid with the excess paper extending over the lower edge. Snip the edge as before and stick the tabs to the inside of the box lid.

To cover the base, cut a strip of paper 4cm (1½in) wider than the depth of the box and long enough to fit round it with a 1cm (⅜in) overlap. Glue this to the box with an equal overlap at the top and bottom. Snip both edges as before and glue the tabs to the inside and base of the box. If desired, glue a circle of paper over the bottom of the box to cover the tabs.

This super box, covered as described here and on page 71, makes a wonderful Christmas gift and can be used for storage long after the contents have been eaten or played with.

Pocket Love

Mention paper crafting and most people think about greetings cards with fixed decorations, but there's so much more to it than that. Take paper pockets, for example. These can be made in a number of ways to create pockets of different shapes and sizes and for different purposes. Here they are used to store decorative tags in a birth-record pocket book, but they could also be used to house memorabilia, such as a baby's hospital tag or a lock of hair.

The pockets shown on the baby pocket book run straight across the front with a slightly shaped back section. There's no need to make them elaborate because the tags inside provide the decorations. But because making pockets in different shapes is fun, there are two alternative designs for you to try – a diamond and a waterfall pocket – for a wedding invitation and a Christmas-tree decoration.

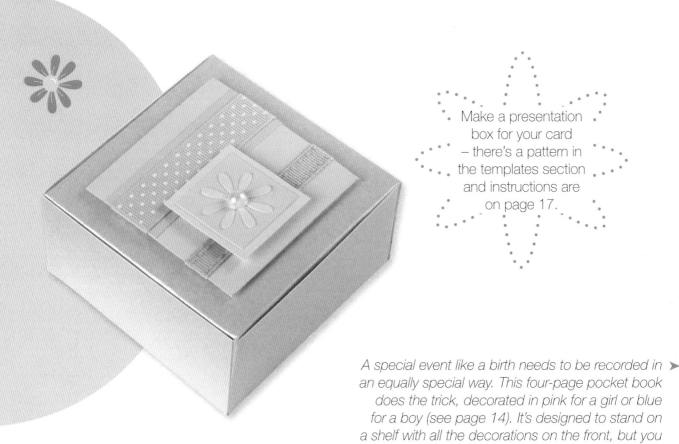

Make a presentation box for your card – there's a pattern in the templates section and instructions are on page 17.

A special event like a birth needs to be recorded in ➤ an equally special way. This four-page pocket book does the trick, decorated in pink for a girl or blue for a boy (see page 14). It's designed to stand on a shelf with all the decorations on the front, but you can add pockets to the other side too if you need additional space.

Baby Girl Pocket Book

Decorated with ribbon, punched daisies and pearl gems, this pretty pocket book could be kept as a personal memento or sent to grandparents or godparents as a wonderful gift. The card features a photograph of the baby, but if this is a gift you could use a picture of the recipient with the baby or tuck additional photographs into the pockets.

● You will need

- Baby photo 7.4 x 9cm (3 x 3½in)

- Three pieces of textured cream card 15.25 x 7.5cm (6 x 3in)

- Two 7.5cm (3in) squares and a 5 x 2cm (2 x ¾in) strip of pink pearlescent card

- Double-sided pink card, 15.25 x 12.5cm (6 x 5in) for a pocket plus 7.4 x 9cm (3 x 3½in) for a picture frame and extra card for the tags

- Double-sided lemon card, 15.25 x 12.5cm (6 x 5in) for a pocket plus 8.5 x 10cm (3⅜ x 4in) for a picture matt and extra card for the tags

- White pearlescent card, 21 x 29.5cm (8⅜ x 11¼in)

- White card for the tags

- 30.5cm (12in) of 1cm (⅜in) wide pink grosgrain ribbon

- 30.5cm (12in) of 1.5cm (⅝in) wide yellow grosgrain ribbon

- 60cm (24in) of 1cm (⅜in) wide lemon organza ribbon

- Four pink organza ribbon bows

- Four lime green brads

- Seven small pearl gems

- Three large pearl gems

- Large and small daisy design punches

- Basic tool kit

- Book size: 30 x 7.5cm
- (12 x 3in) unfolded
- Template is provided on page 100

The girl's book is a brilliant excuse for some really pretty decorations – punched flowers, pearls, ribbons and bows all have a place here.

Make a boy's version of the pocket book from papers in white, blue and green, and instead of daisies for the decorations use a sheet of rub-ons with baby motifs such as a pram, bottle and rubber duck. Keep the decorations fairly simple, building up colour by matting one card onto another.

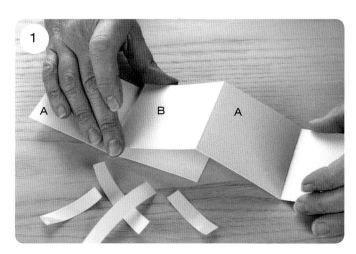

Fold two of the 15.25 x 7.5cm (6 x 3in) rectangles of cream textured card in half with right sides together (A); fold the remaining rectangle in half with wrong sides together (B). Use double-sided tape to glue the rectangles together in the order ABA to make a four-panelled card.

Turn the book over and use double-sided tape to attach the lemon organza ribbon to the centre of the front cover. Glue a 7.5cm (3in) square of pink pearlescent card over the ribbon and another to the back cover.

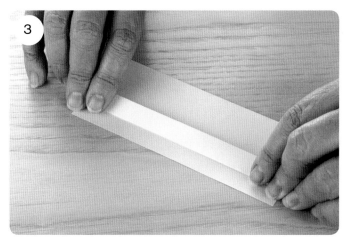

Fold the 15.25 x 12.5cm (6 x 5in) lemon rectangle in half so it is 15.25 x 6.25cm (6 x 2½in). Now fold over 12mm (½in) along the front edge.

Turn the rectangle over and arrange it as shown. Mark the centre of the fold with a pencil. Fold up the bottom edge so it is just short of the pencil line.

Fold over the opposite edge so it overlaps the first edge by 1cm (⅜in). Position as shown. Fold over the top two corners diagonally. Unfold the corners.

Scrapbooking packs

For any project like this where you need a range of coordinating papers, stickers and so on, look out for packs available from scrapbook suppliers, which contain much of what you need.

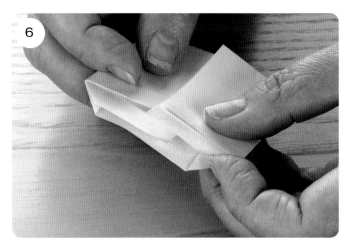

6

7

Reverse fold the diagonal corners by tucking the point inside, as shown. Now slip the right side of the pocket under the left side and the right flap over the left flap. A touch of glue or double-sided tape will help secure the pocket, if needed. Repeat steps 3–6 with the pink 15.25 x 12.5cm (6 x 5in) rectangle.

Fasten a length of pink grosgrain ribbon to the edge of the lemon pocket. Punch a large daisy from white pearlescent card and stick a large pearl gem in the centre. Stick the daisy to the front of the yellow pocket.

8

9

Decorate the pink pocket with a length of yellow grosgrain ribbon. Punch three small daisies from white pearlescent card and stick a small pearl gem in the centre. Stick the daisies to the ribbon, spacing them equally. Now glue the pockets to the two centre pages of the book, using the photograph on page 14 as a guide.

Cut a rectangle from the centre of the pink card to fit your photograph and tie it with a length of pink grosgrain ribbon. Fasten a photograph in the frame and matt it to a piece of lemon card, leaving a 3mm (⅛in) border. Glue a small daisy to the top-left corner, again with a pearl gem in the centre, and glue the whole picture to the inside front page. Make the tags, referring to the pictures below.

Making the Tags

1 Cut four tags using the template on page 100. Glue coordinating ribbons to the tags using double-sided tape – or buy sticky-backed ribbons, which are really easy to use.

2 Matt layers of pink and lemon card and glue a daisy to the centre, topped with a pearl gem. It's quick and easy to do but looks great.

3 Attach a pink organza ribbon bow with a lime green brad to each tag as a finishing touch.

4 You'll want the baby's name on one of the tags. This name was printed on a computer, but you could write the details with a pen. Add other messages to the backs of the tags.

Matching Card Box

You will need

Pink pearlescent card
19 x 30.5cm (7½ x 12in)

Double-sided lemon card
7cm (2¾in) and 3cm (1⅛in) square

Pink double-sided card
2.5 x 7cm (1 x 2¾in)

White pearlescent card
3.5cm (1½in) square

8cm (3⅛in) of 1cm (⅜in) wide pink
grosgrain ribbon

8cm (3⅛in) of 1.5cm (⅝in)
wide yellow grosgrain ribbon

Large daisy punched from
white pearlescent card with
a pearl gem in the centre

Basic tool kit

Box size: 9 x 9 x 4.5cm
(3½ x 3½ x 1⅞in)

Template is provided on
page 101

This box is perfect for storing the baby girl pocket book, or if this is to be a gift, it makes a wonderful presentation box.

Use the template on page 101 to cut out the box from pink pearlescent card. Score and fold along the score lines and fasten the tabs in place with double-sided tape.

Matt the strip of pink card to the large square of lemon card, 1cm (⅜in) from the left-hand side and fasten on the lengths of ribbon. Matt the remaining square of lemon card to the square of white pearlescent card, glue the daisy in the centre and use sticky pads to fasten it towards the bottom-right corner of the square of lemon card. Fix the decorated card to the box lid with sticky pads.

Make a box for the boy's book in the same way but use white card decorated all over with baby rub-ons.

Celebrate the difference

You can use pockets for a host of different paper-crafting projects, not least on your scrapbooking pages, but if you want to try something altogether different, what about the ideas shown here? Full instructions for making the required pockets are given opposite.

- Card size: 7 x 16.5cm (2¾ x 6½in)

Wedding Invitation

Make your own wedding invitation and enclose a blank card that the recipient can use for their reply. If desired, you can also add directions to the venue. And if you aren't getting married, don't miss out – this card could easily be adapted for a party or dinner invitation.

3 Cut a 6.5 x 12cm (2½ x 4¾in) rectangle of silver card and a 5.5 x 11.5cm (2¼ x 4½in) rectangle of white card. Punch the corners of the white card with a decorative corner punch and then matt the white card to the centre of the silver card. Glue two silver die-cut bells together, pierce a hole at the top and fasten the bells to the invitation with a decorative brad.

1 Make a diamond-fold pocket from a 15.25cm (6in) square of spotted vellum, as explained opposite. Use vellum tape to stick the bottom edges and the diamond together and glue a silver die-cut heart to the centre of the diamond.

2 Cut a 7 x 16.5cm (2¾ x 6½in) white card rectangle and print the wedding invitation to fit. Glue the invitation to the card. Now slip this inside the vellum pocket.

Christmas Tree Decoration

There should always be presents under the Christmas tree, and this little hanging Christmas tree, which can be attached to the branch of the real tree, is no exception. It has a little pocket at the base into which you can slip a chocolate coin or other mini delight for little hands to discover.

- Card size: 15 x 11cm (6 x 4¼in)
- Template is provided on page 101

1 Create a waterfall-fold pocket using a 15cm (6in) square of Christmas patterned paper, as explained opposite. Cover the inside of the pocket and the first folded triangle with red paper. Insert a bow-shaped brad to fasten the triangles and glue the open sides together.

3 Knot the ends of a length of gold thread and twist round the back of the brad bow. Glue the tree and trunk to a piece of green card and cut round the edge. Now insert the card in the pocket. You can use a little glue to stick the back of the tree to the back of the pocket.

2 Using the templates on page 101, cut the tree from green card and the trunk from brown card. Decorate the tree with red brads, gold star confetti and a brad bow at the top.

Alternative pocket folds

Here are two ways to create paper or thin card pockets, and these are used for the projects opposite. These pockets can also be added to cards, books or albums.

Folding a Diamond Pocket

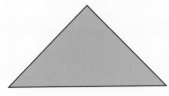

1 Fold a 15cm (6in) square of paper in half diagonally with wrong sides together, to make a triangle.

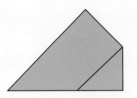

2 With the fold at the bottom, fold the right side of the triangle so that the point is just beyond the centre of the bottom fold.

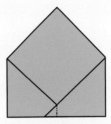

3 Repeat with the left side so that it overlaps the opposite point slightly. Fold the point back to the left along the centre line (marked as a broken line in the diagram).

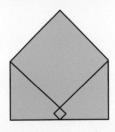

4 Open out the end and push upwards to make a diamond shape. Glue the bottom edges and the diamond shape together to complete the pocket.

Folding a Waterfall Pocket

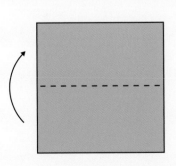

1 Fold a 15cm (6in) square of paper in half with wrong sides together.

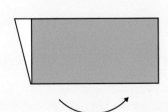

2 Fold in half again from side to side to make a square.

3 Turn the square so that the open edges are facing upwards.

4 Fold the top layer of paper down to end 8mm (¼in) above the bottom point.

5 Repeat with the second layer. You can fold the next layer down too, if required. Now glue the sides together to make the pocket.

Wonder Folds

With a few simple folds, gleaned from origami, you can turn a rectangle of paper or thin card into a panelled house card, which is ideal for people who are moving into a new home, retiring to the country or who simply like homes and gardens. Clever use of thread, beads and gems enhances the three-dimensional effect to make a truly spectacular card.

You'll also find an alternative house card here, which is folded in a slightly different way, giving more space around the house for a garden area. And because people don't move house all that often, you'll find some alternative uses for these clever cards, so if you like, you can make them in lots of different ways for many occasions.

Smart panelled double doors hide the cheerful parlour scene inside this delightful card.

This pretty house card has many enticing features: windows made from vellum over cut apertures so the light can shine through; three-dimensional flowers; copper-brad doorknobs; bead and thread detailing and, of course, its intriguing three-dimensional shape.

New Home

With its vellum windows, bright window boxes and cheerful colours, this cleverly folded house-shaped card could not be more welcoming. Sitting on the parlour table behind the double doors, the friendly cat eagerly awaits the new arrivals.

Dry run

The folds for this card aren't difficult, but if you are in any doubt practice first on a sheet of copier paper. In this case you don't even need to cut the paper to size first.

You will need

Two A4 (US letter) sheets of cream watercolour paper

Flower patterned paper 10.5 x 8cm (4⅛ x 3⅛in)

Pink paper 10.5 x 1.5cm (4⅛ x ⅝in)

Cream card 10.5 x 0.7cm (4⅛ x ¼in)

Light brown card 8 x 7cm (3⅛ x 2¾in)

Dark brown card 5 x 7cm (2 x 2¾in)

Grey card 4 x 7cm (1½ x 2¾in)

Red card 11 x 17cm (4⅜ x 6¾in)

Blue card 7 x 6cm (2¾ x 2⅜in)

Green paper 5.5 x 2.5cm (2⅛ x 1in)

Frosted vellum 8 x 6cm (3⅛ x 2⅜in)

Tile-print paper 22 x 12cm (8⅝ x 4¾in)

Small paper flowers in assorted colours

Eight yellow seed beads size 9 for the flower centres

Two green seed beads size 9 for the cat's eyes

Small pink gemstone for the cat's nose

Black thread for the cat's whiskers

Small black ribbon bow for the cat

Two copper-coloured brads

Basic tool kit

Card size: 21 x 15cm (8¼ x 5¾in)

Templates are provided on page 102

Fold a sheet of cream watercolour paper in half with the long edges together. Mark the centre with a faint pencil line and then fold the outside edges in to meet at the centre line, as shown.

Fold down the top-right edge of the left-hand flap to meet the left side fold. Repeat to fold the top-left edge of the right-hand flap over to meet the right side fold, as shown.

Open out the left flap and make a reverse fold to create the roof shape. Repeat with the right flap and flatten out the card.

Glue the pink paper to the inside of the card level with the lower edge. Glue the floral paper above it – the top edge should be level with the roofline. Glue the cream strip on top, level with the top edge of the pink paper to create the skirting board.

Using the templates on page 102, cut the table from light brown card. Cut the table rim, centre medallion and base separately and glue in place on the table. Now glue the table to the centre of the card, just above the bottom edge.

Cut the cat from grey card. For the eyes glue on two green beads and add a pink gemstone for the nose.

Cat alternative

If the card's recipient doesn't like cats, you can easily replace it with another motif such as a vase of flowers or even a small photograph in a card frame.

Glue the cat on top of the table and use a pricking tool to make eight holes for the whiskers. Place two holes on each side of the nose and two holes on each side of the face where the ends of the whiskers will be.

Stitch the whiskers using one strand of black cotton, knotting the thread end and securing the knot on the back of the card with sticky tape. Push the needle through the holes already made to make the whiskers. When you have stitched all four whiskers, secure the thread with sticky tape at the back. Glue on the ribbon bow as a finishing touch.

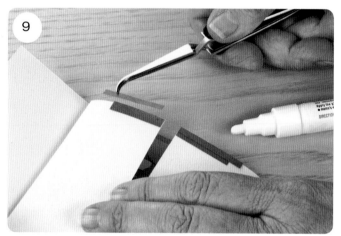

For the doorsteps, cut two dark brown strips 6 x 32mm (¼ x 1¼in) and two dark brown strips 4 x 38mm (⅛ x 1½in). Glue the shortest strips to the inner front edges of the card level with the front and bottom edges. Glue the longer strips on top, as shown.

Using the templates, cut two sets of doors and door panelling from red card and glue panelling to each door. Position the doors above the top step, level with the front edges and glue in place. Make two holes with a perforating tool and attach two brads to make the doorknobs.

Cut a rectangle in each side panel, 2.5 x 4.5cm (1 x 1¾in), 3.5cm (1⅜in) from the bottom and 1.2cm (½in) from the side edges.

Cut window frames from blue card (see page 102) and two pieces of vellum 3.2 x 5cm (1¼ x 2in). Glue the vellum behind the frames and then glue the windows to the window openings on the card.

Cut the window boxes from dark brown card and glue over the windows, matching the bottom edges. Cut two or three green paper flowers into leaf shapes and decorate the window boxes with leaves and flowers, gluing a yellow seed bead to the centre of each flower. Cut some jagged grass from green paper and glue it under the window boxes (see the picture on page 21).

Open out the card. Cut a 21 x 5cm (8¼ x 2in) rectangle of tile-print paper and glue it to the centre section of the roof. Trim the paper level with the diagonals.

Cut two 10.5 x 5cm (4⅛ x 2in) rectangles of tile-print paper. Open the house flaps and glue one rectangle to each house roof; trim along the diagonals level with the card, as before.

Paper choice

Doll's house suppliers are good sources for papers suitable for this card, including the tile print paper for the roof.

Cut out the chimney from red card and glue it to the back of the roof on the left side. Use pieces of cream paper to cover the brads and thread at the back of the card.

House and Garden

This card takes you on a journey down a winding path to the door of a country cottage. Flowers cut from patterned paper have stems stitched in green thread and the garden has small flowers with beaded centres scattered over the lawn. This time, the folding technique gives a feeling of secrecy to the project.

You will need

One A4 sheet of cream watercolour paper

Blue card 16.5 x 15cm (6½ x 6in)

Green paper 10 x 18cm (4 x 7in)

Cream card 7cm (2¾in) square

Light brown card 8 x 5cm (3⅛ x 2in)

Dark brown card 4 x 5cm (1½ x 2in)

Grey card 7 x 2cm (2¾ x ¾in)

Red card 3 x 8cm (1¼ x 3⅛in)

Floral paper 4.5 x 10cm (1¾ x 4in) plus two flower motifs cut from another piece of the paper

Bronze-coloured brad

Small paper flowers

Seven yellow seed beads

Green rayon embroidery cotton (floss)

Basic tool kit

Card size: 27 x 15.5cm (10½ x 6in)

Templates are provided on page 102

Cut a 27 x 15.5cm (10½ x 6in) rectangle of cream watercolour paper. Fold over a 4.5cm (1¾in) flap on each side and then flip the paper over and bring the folds into the middle, as shown.

Turn the paper over and mark the fold lines 4.5cm (1¾in) from all four corners and the centre of the top and bottom edges. Fold all four corners diagonally between the marks, to meet at the centre. Make sure you do not fold the front sections of the card.

Open out the corners and reverse fold them by tucking in the point. Turn the card over to the right side.

Cover the inside of the card, referring to the templates on page 102 to cut the background from blue card and the grass from green paper; glue in place.

Using the templates on page 102, cut the cottage from cream card, the roof from light brown, the windows from grey and the shutters, door and chimney from red card. Glue the pieces of the cottage together starting with the roof, followed by the chimney, door, windows and shutters. Use a bradawl or perforating tool to make a hole in the door and insert a brad to make the doorknob.

Use dark brown card to cut out the path and glue the cottage and path in place. Cut a green paper flower into leaf shapes and glue the flowers and leaves to the grass. Add a yellow seed bead to the centre of each flower.

Cover the left front panel with blue card and glue the two cut-out flowers to the panel. Make holes directly under the flowers and another directly below the right-hand one near the bottom. Stitch the stem using the holes. Secure the thread at the back with tape. Cut the grass from green paper and glue to the front over the flower stem. Work another flower stem as before.

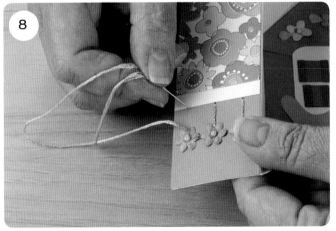

Glue the floral paper to the bottom of the right front panel with a 4.5 x 5cm (1¼ x 2in) piece of green paper above it. Cut a 6 x 45mm (¼ x 1¾in) strip of cream card and glue edge to edge with the flower patterned paper. Glue three paper flowers to the green card, 2cm (⅞in) from the top edge, with a bead in the centre. Use six strands of rayon embroidery cotton to work the stems, making the holes first as before. Line the back and two inside panels of the card with cream watercolour paper to cover the stitching and brad.

Celebrate the difference

The wonder-fold technique is easily adapted to create other house and building scenes or indeed for any purpose that requires three distinct panels. A nativity scene, as shown below, is a wonderful idea, or you could show just one wall of a building as in the tool-shed card opposite. The tool-shed wall could easily be turned into an office, sewing room, artist's studio, potting shed or any other specialized area suited to the recipient.

Nativity Card

It's nice to see a traditional nativity card, and one that has been hand crafted is even more special. To enhance the barn theme, straw-patterned paper is used for the crib and roof and wood-grain paper for the walls, while the outside scenes are decorated with a navy and gold glitter paper.

Card size: 21 x 15cm (8¼ x 5¾in)

Templates are provided on page 103

1 Follow the folding instructions on pages 22–23, steps 1–3, to make a card from a thin A4 sheet of medium brown card. Cover the inside panel with a 10.5 x 8cm (4⅛ x 3⅛in) rectangle of wood-grain paper.

6 Trim a cocktail stick to 5cm (2in) and colour it with a gold pen. Glue two 4cm (1½in) gold die-cut stars together with the cocktail stick in between and use tape to fix the star to the centre back of the card. Cover the back panel with a piece of brown card to finish.

2 Cover the inside flaps up to the roof line with wood-grain paper. Using the template on page 103, cut two doors from dark brown white-core card. Glue these on top, slightly above the bottom edge, but matching the front edges.

5 Cover the roof with straw-patterned paper, following steps 14–15 on page 25.

4 Use the template on page 103 to cut out the pieces for Mary, baby Jesus and the crib, referring to the photograph here for the colours. Glue the pieces in place and draw the eyes, mouth and feature lines with a pencil.

3 Cover the outside panels up to the roofline with navy and gold glitter paper. Cut the grass from green watercolour paper and the palm trees from light green and dark brown white-core card. Add two or three small gold confetti stars to the sky on each side.

In His Shed

Any hard-working man about the house would be delighted with this super card, made from cream card and wood-grain paper, which is embellished with tool stickers. It would work equally well for a garden enthusiast – just use plant pots, forks and trowels instead of the tools.

● Card size: 27 x 15.5cm (10½ x 6in)

● Templates are provided on page 103

1 Stick wood-grain paper to cream card and then follow steps 1–3 for House and Garden on pages 26–27 to make the basic card. Use the templates on page 103 to cut the workbench from brown card. Add 5mm (¼in) wide strips of brown card for the bench legs. Glue these pieces to the inside panel of the card.

2 To make the view, cut a 5.5 x 6.5cm (2¼ x 2½in) rectangle of mid blue card. Cut a 5.5 x 2.5cm (2¼ x 1in) green strip and glue it to the blue card, matching the bottom edges. Using the templates, cut a dark green tree and a dark brown trunk and assemble on the background. Punch some circles of orange card for fruits and stick these on too.

3 Cut a 5.5 x 6.5cm (2¼ x 2½in) rectangle of acetate and brown card. Cut a 4.5 x 5cm (1¾ x 2in) window in the centre of the brown card to make the window frame. Now cut a 4.5 x 5cm (1¾ x 2in) window in the centre of the main card, 6mm (¼in) above the workbench. Use double-sided tape to fasten the acetate to the window frame and then to the window scene. Fit the window over the opening in the main card with the bottom of the windowsill level with the top of the workbench.

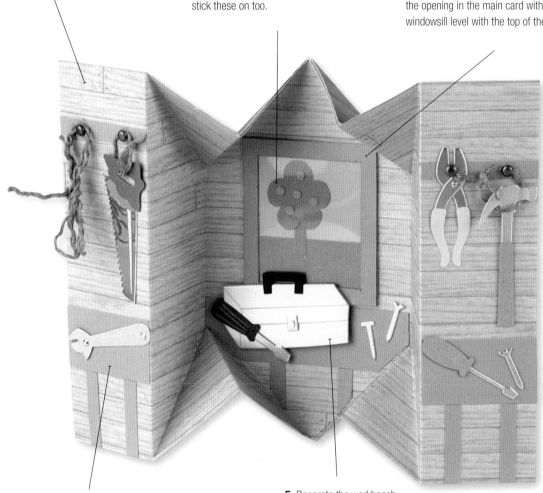

4 Glue a 4.5 x 2.5cm (¾ x 1in) strip of brown card to each front side panel, parallel with the inside workbench and make the legs from 0.5 x 3cm (¼ x 1¼in) strips of brown card. Cut two 4.5 x 0.5cm (1¾ x ¼in) strips from brown card and glue these to the top of the side panels, 3cm (1¼in) and 2cm (¾in) from the top edges. Use brads to attach tool stickers hung from lengths of string to the strips of card and then make a rope from twisted string and attach this too.

5 Decorate the workbench with tool stickers.

Boxing Clever

Some gifts just don't want to be wrapped, or so it seems, but this trio of boxes should help make things easier, and they look great too. Each one is made from a template that you simply cut, fold and then decorate, so it couldn't be easier. The templates are for small boxes that you could fill with sweets or other little gifts and hang on a Christmas tree, but you can enlarge the patterns to make bigger versions as required.

With a little lateral thinking, you could use these boxes at other times of year too. Change the colours and decorations, and perhaps add a few extra pieces cut from card to create something for a special birthday. You'll find some suggestions on page 35, where there's even a special back-to-school box to ensure you're top of the class.

Good packaging makes all the difference. Wouldn't you love to receive this gift?

Hanging sweets from the Christmas tree is a long-standing tradition in many cultures. Introduce some mystery and suspense by hiding goodies inside these intriguing boxes. What's in the box? It could be chocolate liquors, shortcake biscuits, a muffin, nuts or even a small toy.

Star Top Box

Cut from a single piece of red card and decorated with metallic card, confetti stars and glitter, this box is deceptively easy to make. The unusual shape really catches the eye and the recipient won't have any idea what's inside.

You will need

- 30.5cm (12in) square of red card
- Scraps of green and gold metallic card
- Glue Line
- Gold glitter
- Four medium-sized gold confetti stars
- 35cm (14in) of 5mm (³⁄₁₆in) wide gold ribbon
- Medium-sized star punch (optional)
- Basic tool kit

Box size at the widest point: 8 x 8 x 10cm (3 x 3 x 4in)

Templates are provided on page 104

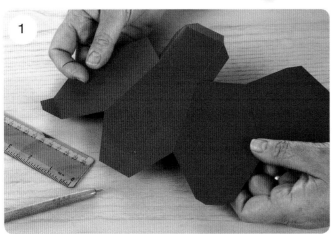

1 Trace the Star Top Box template on page 104 and cut it out from red card. Score and fold along the fold lines and flatten out the card on your work surface.

2 Fasten a strip of Glue Line to the top of each side, 7mm (¼in) from the edge. Remove the backing paper, sprinkle with gold glitter and dust off the excess.

3 Using the template on page 104, cut four triangles from green metallic card and glue one to each side with a gold confetti star at the top. Now you can fasten the box together using double-sided tape.

4 Cut or punch four stars from gold metallic card. Take two stars and glue them back to back with one of the tabs at the top of the box in between. Repeat to glue stars to the opposite pair of tabs. Insert your gift and then tie the stars together with the gold ribbon.

Pyramid Box

There is something mysterious and intriguing about the pyramid shape, which is why it makes such a satisfying gift box. It's also perfect for those awkward presents like bottles with stoppers that are usually so horrible to wrap.

You will need

30.5cm (12in) square of red card

Scraps of green metallic card

Glue Line

Gold glitter

One large and two medium-sized gold confetti stars

Two 22cm (8¾in) lengths of 5mm (³⁄₁₆in) wide gold ribbon

Small Christmas-tree punch

Basic tool kit

Box size at the base: 8 x 8 x 10cm (3 x 3 x 4in)

Templates are provided on page 104

Trace the Pyramid Box template on page 104 and cut it out from red card. Score and fold along the fold lines and flatten out the card on your work surface. Decorate each panel with a line of gold glitter as explained in step 2 for the Star Top Box. Now punch ten Christmas trees from green metallic card. Glue these to one panel, as shown, and add a gold confetti star at the top. Repeat on the opposite panel.

For the tag cut a large red card triangle and a smaller green triangle using the templates provided. Glue the green triangle centrally on the red one. Add a large gold confetti star near the top and then make a gold glitter strip along the bottom as before. Punch a hole at the top for a tie.

Punch a hole at the top of each of the four triangles and thread the lengths of ribbon through the holes from side to side, as shown.

Festive punch

If you don't have a small Christmas-tree punch you could use any festive shapes, such as bells or angels or you could even use star stickers.

Insert your gift and then tie the ribbon together in an overhand knot to close the box. Thread the tag on one of the ends and secure with a knot.

Chocolate Box

This may be a very straightforward box shape compared with the previous two, but it's also very useful. It will fit onto a standard A4 (US letter) sheet of paper, but if you can get your hands on some bigger sheets you can easily enlarge it to hold CDs, DVDs, books, pictures and more.

You will need

Red card 21 x 25cm (8¼ x 9¾in)

Scraps of green and gold metallic card

Glue Line

Gold glitter

45cm (18in) length of 5mm (³⁄₁₆in) wide gold ribbon

Red eyelet

Small Christmas-tree punch

Medium-sized star punch (optional)

Basic tool kit

Box size: 7 x 7 x 2cm (2¾ x 2¾ x ¾in)

Templates are provided on page 105

1

Trace the Chocolate Box template on page 105 and cut it out from red card. Score and fold along the fold lines and flatten out the card on your work surface. Fasten a strip of Glue Line to the front panel of the box and add glitter as in step 2 for the Star Top Box (see page 32).

2

Punch five green metallic Christmas trees using your tree punch and stick these to the front panel of the box just above the glitter line. Space the trees as evenly as possible.

3

Thread the ribbon through the two slits at the back of the box, as shown. Fold the box together, insert your gift and fasten the box with the large tabs.

4

Cut or punch two gold metallic stars and glue them together back to back to make the tag. Insert an eyelet into one of the points of the star, thread it with one of the ribbon ends and then tie a bow with both ends.

Celebrate the difference

Boxes are useful throughout the year, not just at Christmas, so here are some suggestions for adapting the boxes for different purposes.

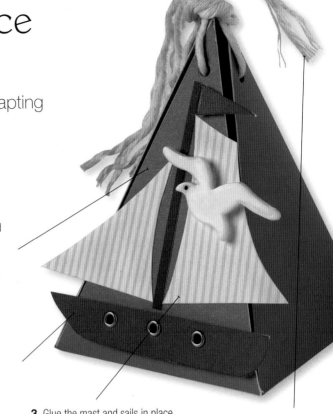

Boating for Boys

This sailing boat, with its super eyelet portholes, fits brilliantly onto the front of the pyramid box. Choose a mid blue for the main box to suggest the sea and sky.

1 Trace the Pyramid Box template on page 104 and cut it out from blue card. Score and fold the box as instructed on page 33 but don't assemble it yet.

2 Use the templates on page 105 to cut the boat pieces. Fix three copper-coloured eyelets along the side of the hull and then fix the hull to the box front with sticky pads.

3 Glue the mast and sails in place and attach the flag with another sticky pad. Remove the shank from a sea gull button and glue it to the sail.

4 Thread cord or string through the holes and assemble the box to finish.

Back To School Satchel

Chase away those back-to-school blues with this delightful gift. Fill it with little messages of encouragement, sweets (if allowed) or tuck money and perhaps add the name of the child to the front for that personalized touch.

1 Trace the Chocolate Box template on page 105 and cut it out from pale green card (or the school colours), making the two slits at the back, 2cm (¾in) wide. Score and fold the box but don't assemble it yet.

2 Cut a strip of black card 2 x 24cm (¾ x 9½in). Cut a strip of green card 1.3 x 24cm (½ x 9½in) and glue it centrally on top. When dry, trim one end to a point. Using the template on page 105, cut the buckle from black card. Thread the point of the strip through the slits at the back of the box and fold the strip around the box. Attach the buckle to the strip and glue it in place, as shown.

3 Cut a 2 x 9cm (¾ x 3½in) strip of black card and stick a 1.3 x 9cm (½ x 3½in) strip of green card centrally on top. Trim one end to a point and attach a black card buckle to the other end. Glue the pointed end to the side of the box.

4 For the other part of the handle cut a 2 x 15cm (¾x 6in) strip of black card and stick a 1.3 x 15cm (½x 6in) strip of green card centrally on top. Trim both ends to a point and stick one end to the free side of the box. Thread the free end of the strip through the buckle.

5 Complete the decorations by cutting out four black corner pieces and sticking these in place.

Picture This

Iris folding is an easy paper-folding technique that's fun for all the family. It is worked directly over a template and all you have to do is layer pre-folded strips along the template lines in number order. Because so many layers are used, the technique is traditionally worked with fairly thin papers such as origami paper, but in practice almost any paper can be used, and if you are keen to recycle, the insides of envelopes, seed catalogues and newspapers make ideal material.

Mostly iris folding is used to decorate cards. Cards are useful, and any of the designs here can be used in this way, but it's fun to think of other ideas, which is why the champagne-glass design is used on the cover of a wedding album. Other ideas include decorations for a memory box and gift bag (see pages 40 and 41).

This beautiful design could easily be used for a card or tag.

The cover of an album is almost as important as its ➤ *contents because it gives the first impression. This unusual iris-fold design sets just the right note of celebration for a wedding.*

Silver Wedding Album

Folded strips of vellum are used for the iris folding in this design and create just the right combination of luxury and sophistication. A silver spine and silver peel-off stars add sparkle to the occasion.

Careful sticking

Make sure you don't get any sticky tape inside the champagne-glass window where it will show, and ensure you don't extend it onto the work surface either as it might stick and pull your vellum off the card.

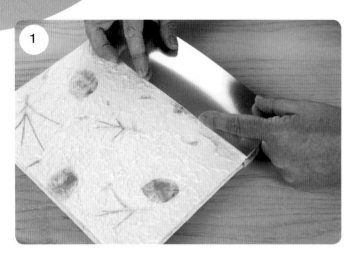

Use the handmade flower-petal paper to cover the photograph album as explained on page 8. Alternatively, you may be able to buy an album already covered in a suitable paper. Glue the strip of thin silver metallic card round the spine and leave to dry.

Trace the outline of the champagne glass from page 106 onto the white embossed card, positioning it 1.5cm (⅝in) above the bottom edge and evenly spaced between the side edges. Place the card on a cutting mat and cut out the shape with a sharp craft knife. Use a low-tack tape to fasten the card in position over the template, wrong side up.

You will need

- **Photograph album – this one is 19 x 25cm (7½ x 10in)**
- **Sheet of handmade flower-petal paper**
- **White embossed card 10 x 15cm (4 x 6in)**
- **Silver mirror card 11 x 16cm (4¼ x 6¼in)**
- **Thin silver metallic card to fit round the spine**
- **Two 30.5cm (12in) lengths of pink vellum, 2.5cm (1in) wide**
- **Two 30.5cm (12in) lengths of peach vellum, 2.5cm (1in) wide**
- **Small silver peel-off stars**
- **Decorative corner punch**
- **Basic tool kit**

- Design size including the silver matt: 11 x 16cm (4¼ x 6¼in)
- Template is provided on page 106

Fold each of the vellum strips in half lengthways with wrong sides together. Crease each fold with a bone folder.

4

Beginning at the bottom of the glass, place a folded strip of peach vellum up to the line of section A. The folded edge should be facing inwards towards the section marked C. Trim off the excess vellum so it extends by about 5mm (3⁄16in) on each side and then stick the strip to the back of the white card with tiny pieces of sticky tape.

5

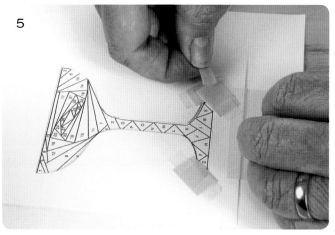

Repeat the process to stick a strip of vellum over section B, again with the fold towards the inside. When you add piece C it will overlap piece A, which is fine. As before, make sure the folded edge is facing inwards.

6

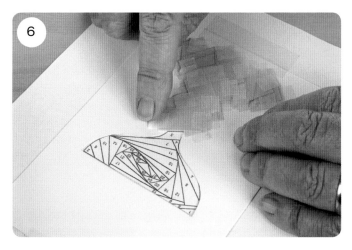

Continue to use the folded peach vellum strips, working alphabetically until you have covered all the lettered sections.

7

Now change to a folded pink vellum strip and start at 1 to fill in the top of the glass. Work in number order, making sure that the folded edge faces inwards.

8

When you finish at section 29 there will be a tiny triangle remaining at the centre. Stick a piece of double thickness vellum over this triangle to finish.

9

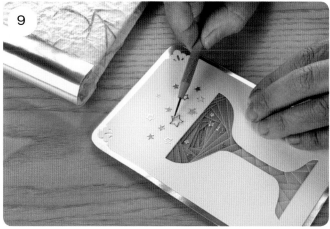

Remove the low-tack tape and turn the design over to reveal the finished effect. Punch the corners of the white card with the decorative corner punch. Round off the corners of the silver mirror card and glue the iris-fold design in the centre. Add small silver star peel-offs, some in the glass and some just above it, to make the 'bubbles'. Now glue the design to the centre front of the album.

Celebrate the difference

Any item that can be decorated with a paper shape can be embellished with an iris-fold design. Think of tags and cards, boxes, bags and folders, albums, books and so on. You can even frame one or combine several in a large design. To inspire you, here's one design for a child and another for a man.

Baby Memory Box

Little children – and bigger ones too – love to have somewhere to store things, and this box is ideal. The peachy colouring is suitable for a boy or girl, or for a grown-up starting a collection for a baby, though you can easily change the colours to suit the child. The design is built around a ready-made box, so start saving some of that packaging.

- Box size: 11.5 x 5 x 19cm (4½ x 2 x 7½in)
- Template is provided on page 106

2 Cut a 10 x 17.5cm (4 x 6⅞in) rectangle of cream textured card for the teddy aperture. Trace the teddy from page 106 onto the cream card 3.5cm (1⅜in) from the top; cut it out. Using the template on page 106 and referring to the instructions on pages 38–39, arrange four different folded papers behind the aperture, finishing with a piece of dark peach card in the centre topped with a small red confetti heart. Stick the completed teddy bear to a rectangle of dark peach card and trim the edges to leave a narrow peach border.

1 Cover a box with two different patterned papers as explained on page 10 – this box is 11.5 x 5 x 19cm (4½ x 2 x 7½in). Glue a 1.5cm (⅝in) wide strip of cream ribbon around the edge of the lid and decorate it with small teddy bears, punched from the same paper that you used to cover the lid.

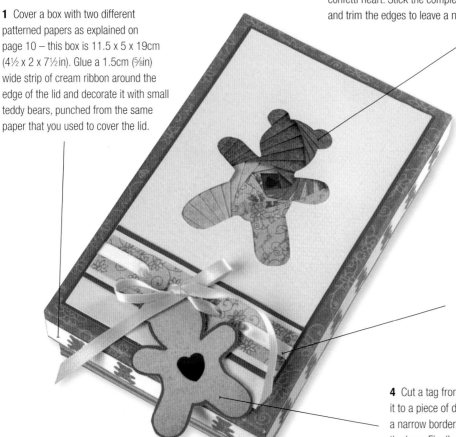

3 Cut a 10 x 3cm (4 x 1¼in) strip of dark peach card. Onto this matt a 10 x 2.5cm (4 x 1in) strip of cream card and on top of that matt a 10 x 2cm (4 x ¾in) strip of patterned paper. Punch four evenly spaced holes in the strip. Cut two 25cm (10in) lengths of matching 6mm (¼in) wide cream satin ribbon. Thread through the holes, to meet at the centre and secure at the back of the strip with sticky tape. Glue the teddy bear to the box lid then glue the ribboned strip below the teddy.

4 Cut a tag from plain paper using the pattern on page 106. Stick it to a piece of dark peach card and trim around the edge, leaving a narrow border. Glue a large red confetti heart to the tummy of the bear. Finally, punch a hole in one of the ears, thread it with the ribbon and tie in a bow.

Men's Gift Bag

Your Father's Day gift will be gratefully received in this gift bag decorated with a classic car shape. Frame the picture afterwards and hang it on the wall. Keep the car bright and graphic by using just one colour for all the iris-paper folds. Add detail to the wheels with a brad and finish with a card frame.

- Framed image size: 18 x 12cm (7 x 4¾in)
- Template is provided on page 106

For a child
Adapt this gift bag for a child by using the teddy motif, opposite, and a bright paper bag.

1 Cut a 17 x 12cm (6¾ x 4¾in) piece of textured cream card for the car aperture. Trace the car motif from page 106 onto the wrong side of the card; cut it out. Using the template on page 106 and referring to the instructions on pages 38–39, arrange folded strips of dull red metallic paper to the back of the aperture.

2 For the wheels cut or punch circles of black card and fasten them to the car with silver brads.

3 Cut a 13 x 7cm (5⅛ x 2¾in) aperture in an 18 x 12cm (7 x 4¾in) rectangle of brown ripple card and glue it over the car. Now fix the frame to a brown paper bag – don't use strong glue if you wish to frame it afterwards.

4 Cut a tag from dull red metallic paper, using the pattern on page 106. Make and attach wheels in the same way as before and then glue the car to cream textured card. Trim around the edge, leaving a narrow border. Finally, punch a hole at the top of the tag and tie it to the handle with string.

Card Connections

Artists' Trading Cards (ATCs) originated in the 16th century, when they were painted by portrait artists and sold as wallet 'photos'. The last decade has seen renewed interest in this form of artwork, with any materials or techniques being used to create a card, including stamping, decoupage, collage, stickers and even small needlework or knitted pieces. No longer sold, they are traded between crafters with their details listed on the back like a handcrafted business card, either as individual pieces of art or as part of a themed series.

The travel-themed ATCs shown here are created using basic paper-craft techniques – cutting, tearing and sticking – with additional embellishments provided with stamps, stickers, fibres, buttons and so on. They are presented in a wonderful paper album that has been decorated in the same way. This is a wonderful way of storing the cards, and if you are making several themed sets you can simply string them together with colourful threads, finishing with a few suitable charms (see pages 48–51).

ATCs can be any size but are usually roughly business-card size. These cards are 6.5 x 9cm (2½ x 3½in).

Decorated with historical travel images and coloured with stamps and inkpads to ➤ create a faded look, this album and the cards within it capture the glamour and excitement of travel in years gone by. The album is easy to make from three 17.5cm (7in) squares of paper, or you can make the album with additional pages, if required.

Voyage of a Lifetime Album

This stunning ATC album recalls a time when travel was a luxury and a true adventure. Made from beautiful textured paper, the colours have been enhanced with inkpads, and the whole album completed with some torn paper strips, fibres and a few other embellishments that complement the designs of the cards it contains. The materials listed are sufficient for making both the album and the cards inside.

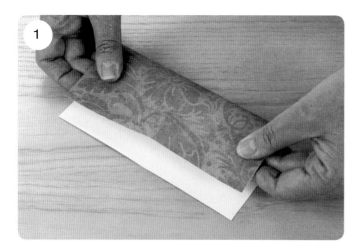

Fold a 17.5cm (7in) square of textured paper in half, wrong sides together, open out and fold in half again the other way, as shown, so that the fold lines cross in the centre.

Fold the two bottom corners diagonally up to the centre.

You will need

- Several sheets of textured paper
- One 20cm (8in) square of beige paper
- Several sheets of cranberry-coloured card
- One A4 sheet of travel-theme paper
- Sheet of bronze ripple card
- Three laser-cut wooden buttons featuring a train, liner and travelling bag
- Travel collage images
- Travel-theme stamp
- Dark brown, light brown, cranberry and dark blue inkpads
- Selection of brown, copper and mulberry coloured ribbons, braids and threads
- Handful of 5mm (3/16in) and 3mm (1/8in) bronze coloured brads
- Sandpaper
- Basic tool kit

- Album page size: 8.75 x 8.75cm (3½ x 3½in)

Turn the square over, rub the diagonal folds with sandpaper and colour the edges with the cranberry inkpad.

Slip sheets of paper between the triangle and the folded paper. Colour the triangle with the cranberry inkpad and use the dark brown inkpad to stamp the travel design.

Rub the edges of the front and back covers with sandpaper and use the cranberry inkpad to colour the covers and edges.

Turn the square over again and fold the point to meet the top edge, as shown.

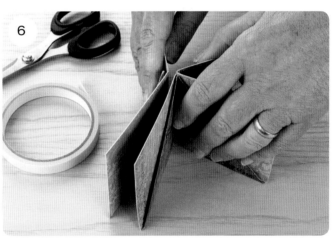

Repeat steps 1–5 with two more squares of textured paper and cover the top of the squares with 17.5 x 9cm (7 x 3½in) rectangles of textured paper. Glue the three pieces together back to back to make the book.

Quick work

If you use double-sided paper there is no need to line the pocket pages (see step 6).

Tear diagonally along one long edge of a 9 x 5cm (3½ x 2in) strip of cranberry-coloured card. Colour and edge with the dark brown inkpad. Glue the card to the front cover, matching the long straight edge to the spine of the book. Glue a smaller torn piece of bronze ripple card on top.

Tearing paper

Tear paper towards you with the right side facing up to create an attractive white border around the edges. If you want to avoid the border, tear paper towards you with the wrong side facing up.

Cut several 50cm (20in) lengths of assorted fibres and use double-sided tape to fasten them diagonally across the front cover.

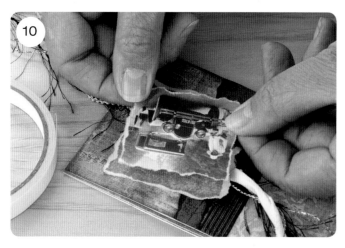

Tear the edges of a 7cm (2¾in) square of textured paper and a slightly smaller travel image. Colour the square, image and edges with the light brown inkpad and glue both pieces over the fibres.

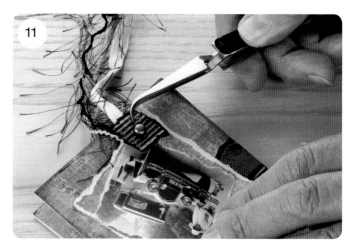

Insert a 3mm (⅛in) brad in the centre of a small torn square of bronze ripple card and fix it over the point at which the fibres emerge.

Planes, Trains and Automobiles

The travel theme is continued with a collection of ATCs that can be stored in the album. Each ATC is based on a 6.5 x 9cm (2½ x 3½in) rectangle of cranberry-coloured card. Once the decorations are complete, you can back your ATCs with textured paper and rectangles of beige paper, torn, coloured and edged with the light brown inkpad.

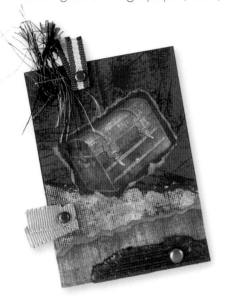

● Card size: 6.5 x 9cm
● (2½ x 3½in)

A travelling-bag image, coloured and edged with the cranberry inkpad and glued to the card at an angle is the main focal point of this card. Fibres and ribbons add further interest along with torn paper strips.

For railway enthusiasts, a train button, coloured with the dark blue inkpad and tied with fibres, makes an unusual centrepiece on this card, applied over criss-crossed layers of ribbon and torn paper.

Here, 14cm (5½in) lengths of ribbons and fibres, knotted in the centre were glued across the centre over a torn-paper background. A small travel image with the edges torn, coloured and edged with the light brown inkpad, was glued on at an angle.

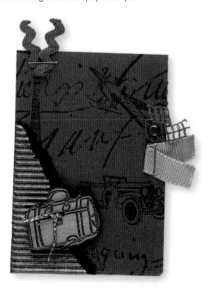

A travel design was stamped onto this cranberry card using the dark brown inkpad and then covered in the bottom-left corner with a torn triangle of bronze ripple card. A travel bag button, coloured with the light brown inkpad and tied with bronze fibre enhances the theme.

A superb image of a liner is the focus here, emphasized by colouring the edges with the dark blue inkpad. This was applied over travel-theme paper and completed with two small torn squares of textured paper, coloured with the light brown inkpad, two large brads and some ribbon.

Reminding us of those magnificent men in their flying machines, this card features an old-fashioned plane. Rickrack braid, glued over bronze-coloured ribbon, picks up on the colours of the plane and the wooden button with its liner image, which has been coloured with the cranberry inkpad.

Celebrate the difference

Making ATCs is fun and because each card is small you can usually snatch the time to make at least one at some point in the day. Here are some additional ATCs to whet your appetite. They are grouped, like the travel ATCs but this time they are simply tied together so they can be presented as a simple gift. Use the same papers for all ATCs in a set to ensure coordination.

Mother's Day Hobby Set

Mother's Day is an opportunity to say 'thank you' to mum for all the things she does, so this set of hobby-theme ATCs covering cross stitch, petit point, dressmaking and knitting is ideal for a mum whose needleworking skills are legendary. The Retro-inspired paper adds flavour to the projects as do the pieces of cross-stitch and petit point, which can be worked following the diagrams provided. Use threads tied with scissor and thimble charms – the 'tools of the trade' – to fasten them together.

- Card size: 6.5 x 9cm (2½ x 3½in)
- Charts and template are provided on page 107

A small cross-stitch embroidery can be presented on an ATC card in a card frame (see the chart on page 107). The frame is 4cm (1⅝in) square with a 3cm (1⅛in) square aperture. Decorate the card before adding the embroidery using coordinating papers and a piece of cross-stitch chart if you can get one. A short length of thread on the back of the picture makes a hanger, which is fixed to the card with a brad.

A miniature knitting sample is perfect for an avid knitter, backed with a sample of knitting pattern printed from your computer. The knitting can be worked on two cocktail sticks using perle cotton. This sample was worked on 14 stitches in garter stitch, finishing in the centre of a row. Trim the excess thread and coil one end, then glue the knitting to the card.

Continuing the craft theme, this card features a tapestry, which has been nearly completed. A hand-coloured chart for the tapestry has been stuck to the card first along with some coordinating papers, and the tapestry and needle glued on top. If preferred, you can omit the needle.

This is ideal for someone who enjoys dressmaking. A simple silhouette of a dressmaker's dummy is the main feature of the card (see templates, page 107) and a hand-stitched strip of paper emphasizes the theme. Make the stitching holes in the paper first to ensure even spacing. The needle can be left in place, as here, or you could cut the thread and tape the thread ends to the back of the paper before gluing it to the card.

In the Garden

This lovely set of ATCs is perfect for a keen gardener. Clever use of floral paper, matching ribbon and printed embellishments, create the perfect themed set. Use your own photographs instead of pictures, to personalize the cards and torn vellum and decoupage to give extra dimension. Butterfly, bee and dragonfly charms, coloured with a permanent pink marker pen, have been knotted onto the ends of a frayed length of garden twine and tied in a knot to hold the cards together.

● Card size: 6.5 x 9cm (2½ x 3½in)

A tag is a nice addition to any paper-craft project, and here it works especially well as it implies a plant label or packet of seeds. Here, the card was covered first with floral paper, with a torn vellum strip over one corner. Decorate a tag and add a decoupage flower. You can give this added dimension by cutting some petals from a second motif and sticking these on top with sticky pads to raise them off the surface. A few dots of gold marker pen will enhance the centre of the flower. Complete the decorations with more decoupage and ribbon trims.

Your ATC designs don't have to be complicated. In this design two layers of cut petals have been placed over a corresponding flower motif using sticky pads to lift them off the surface. A simple ribbon trim and some gold pen on the flower centres are the only additional embellishments.

This card design is based around an image – an idyllic Victorian garden scene – though you could use a family photograph to personalize it. The double mat of green vellum and pink card links the picture to the colours of the floral paper and some cut-out flowers from the paper overlap the background and picture to increase the organic feel of the composition.

Here is another way of presenting an image. It is completed like card 3 but with the mats reversed and with a strip of ribbon running across the card between the mats.

Using eyelets

When joining the cards, insert an eyelet in the top-left corner before threading.

Gone Fishing

What better way to celebrate a retirement than with this authentic group of fishing-inspired ATCs? Rub-ons, nylon line and flies, combined with the subtle brown and green colour scheme, really bring this popular sport to life. To fasten the cards together, knot a fly to each end of a length of nylon line, fold the line in half and push the loop through the eyelets. Thread the ends through the loop and pull them tightly.

- Card size: 6.5 x 9cm (2½ x 3½in)

Get to the point

The fly hooks used to embellish the nylon tying cord are very sharp so file them down before attaching them.

This set of cards is built around a set of rub-ons. Here, a fish and fly have been rubbed onto cream card and then cut out, leaving a narrow border, to create tags. They are attached to the card with short lengths of wire, which are then tied to a hole in the card. Sticky pads under the tags hold them in place and lift them off the surface. Decorate the card with torn paper and ribbon before attaching the tags.

Here, a large rub-on has been applied directly over the decorated card. Three silver brads applied along one side create the bubbles.

Several rub-ons from a sheet can be successfully combined on one card – this can be a good way of using up any leftover rub-ons. Here, one of the fish rub-ons has been mounted on a card background for impact.

A fish stamp is not enough on its own to embellish this card, so it has been combined with rub-ons, torn paper and ribbon. Notice that the large rub-on has been added to cream card and then cut out, as on the first card.

Sports and All

Joined together with a shoelace tied in a bow and embellished with sport-theme peel-offs, these sporting ATCs are great for men and boys. The popular sports of football, tennis, rugby and baseball are brought to life using peel-offs, grass patterned paper and mesh. This set would make an excellent birthday greeting.

- Card size: 6.5 x 9cm (2½ x 3½in)
- Templates are provided on page 107

Grass-effect paper is ideal as the base for a sporting card, but you can't have football without a net. This one is made from a 5 x 3.5cm (2 x 1⅜in) piece of mesh edged with 3mm (⅛in) strips cut from a sticky white label. The football peel-off was stuck to white card first and coloured with a black marker. The templates for the tufts of grass are on page 107.

As on the football card, 3mm (⅛in) wide strips from a sticky white label were used here, this time to create the lines of the court. The net is a 2.5cm (1in) deep rectangle of mesh and the ball and racket are peel-offs applied to white card and coloured in.

The peel-offs on this card have been stuck to paper and coloured in before gluing them to the grass-effect paper. Some simple card shapes complete the effect.

Complete the sports theme with a rugby card, made in the same way as the others in the set.

Echoes of Love

When this clever card is closed it is very pretty, but it looks similar to any standard card – that is until you open it, and open it, and open it. For inside this card are four more pages that have been shaped for added impact. It's a lovely idea, and if anyone else has sent a card, this is the one that will stand out from the rest. After all, what could say 'I love you' more than a string of richly decorated hearts that include hidden photographs or messages?

It's such a good idea that you'll want similar cards for other occasions so on pages 56–57 you'll find three more cards – a baby card, Mother's Day card and young child's card, all made in the same way but with some very different shapes.

The winged heart symbolizes the link between body and soul. 'Where your treasure is, there will your heart be also.'

With photographs or messages hidden behind ➤
folded hearts and further hearts stitched with kisses,
you can be sure he'll get the message with this
super Valentine card.

Valentine Card

It's nice to take time over a Valentine's Day card to show how much you care. This one has plenty going on, with pockets, envelopes, cut-out shapes, folding, stitching and sticking. It's a card to be proud of, and by the time you've finished you may have learnt a few new techniques into the bargain.

Scrap work
Most of the pieces on this card are quite small, so it's a good opportunity to use up scraps and leftovers. See what you have in the way of red and pink card before you go and buy more.

You will need
- **White card 11.5 x 54cm (4½ x 21in)**
- **Sheet of red double-sided card**
- **Scraps of gold and pink card**
- **Sheet of pink glitter card**
- **Sheet of pink metallic card**
- **Pink angel-hair paper 10cm (4in) square**
- **Stranded gold embroidery cotton (floss)**
- **Two sheets of gold heart peel-offs**
- **Sheet of pink and red heart stickers**
- **Gold elastic or ribbon to fasten the card**
- **Basic tool kit**

Card size: 11.5 x 54cm (4½ x 21in)

Templates provided on pages 108–109

With so many surfaces to decorate, this card will be lots of fun to make.

1

Divide the strip of white card into six 9cm (3½in) rectangles and use the heart-shaped book template on page 108 to draw four hearts between the two end rectangles, matching the short straight lines. Cut out along the other lines.

Make a mountain fold along the centre line, valley folds along the lines on either side and two more mountain folds along the two outside lines. Flatten the card out and cover with gold peel-offs.

Trace the keyhole and arrow pockets and cut one each from red card. Cut a key and an arrow from gold card. Push the arrow through the slits, with the fold on the left and glue the key to the left of the keyhole with the fold on the right. Fasten to the first and last heart pages at an angle.

Cut one large wrapped heart each from pink and pink glitter card and a heart frame from pink metallic card. Cut a six-strand length of gold thread, wrap it around the pink glitter heart and fix the ends to the back with sticky tape. Stick a small heart sticker to a piece of card, cut it out and thread with a single strand of gold thread. Tie in a knot and fasten the thread to the back of the heart at the centre. Glue the two large hearts together and fasten to the second heart-shaped page at an angle, with the pink metallic heart on top.

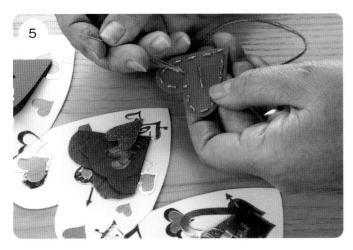

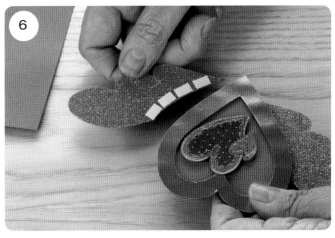

Cut the heart envelope from pink angel-hair paper, two large envelope hearts from pink card and a small heart from pink glitter card. Fold the envelope along the fold lines, stick together with a dab of glue, and decorate with a heart peel-off at the front. Glue to the remaining page, with the pink metallic heart on top. Make holes in one of the pink hearts and use a six-strand length of gold thread to work a row of running stitches around the edge and a cross in the centre, taping the thread ends on the back. Glue to the other pink heart and fasten inside the envelope. Decorate with a small heart sticker.

For the front cover, cut a pair of wings from pink glitter card, a large heart from pink card and a heart frame from pink metallic card. Use sticky pads to fix the pink metallic heart to the pink heart and to fix a heart sticker, stuck to card and cut out, in the centre. Fix the wings to the back of the heart, as shown.

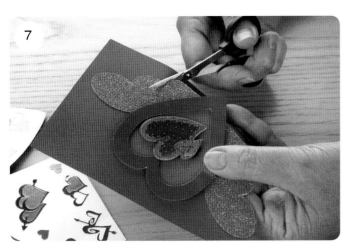

Glue the winged heart to a piece of red card, cut it out and glue it to the left cover of the book at an angle. Fasten the book with lengths of gold elastic or ribbon (see the photograph on page 52).

Keep the shine

Metallic card is easily scratched and smeared so handle it carefully. Once the Valentine card is complete you can buff the metallic card lightly with a soft, clean cloth.

Celebrate the difference

Once you have drawn a simple template, it is easy to create a strip card for any occasion. Here are three ideas, using a 45 x 8cm (18 x 3¾⁶in) strip of card.

Blue for a Boy

Teddies are always popular for children and baby themes. This one is made even more interesting because each teddy is wearing a different outfit. You could repeat the idea for a girl using a doll motif.

● Card size: 45 x 8cm (18 x 3¾⁶in)
●
● Templates are provided on page 109

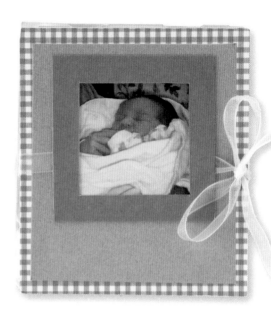

It's twins

This card can easily be adapted for twins. Reduce the number of bear pages down to two and put a photograph on the front and back of the card.

1 Make the card in the same way as the Valentine card on page 54 but using the teddy template from page 109. Cover the front and back covers with green and blue paper.

2 Matt a piece of green card to the front cover and fasten a length of ribbon across the centre. Cut a frame from blue card to fit your photograph, stick the photo in the frame and glue it over the ribbon.

3 Use the patterns on page 109 to cut out the clothes from scraps of card. Use textured cream paper for the nappy. Glue the pieces to the bears and clip a small safety pin to the nappy.

4 Sew small buttons to the braces and romper suit and glue bows of cream stranded cotton to the shoes.

5 Glue wiggly eyes on the bears – these are always popular.

Tulip Birthday Card

This card reflects nostalgically on younger days, whilst maintaining a stylish look – the shape is mature but the insects have a fun, child-like air. For speed, you could use stickers for the insects instead of tracing and colouring them in.

- Card size: 45 x 8cm (18 x 3 3/16 in)
- Templates are provided on page 110

1 Make the card in the same way as the Valentine card on page 54 but using the tulip template from page 110. Stick a length of red grosgrain ribbon to the centre of the front cover then matt the front and back covers with green Canson paper (pastel paper), leaving a narrow border around the edge.

2 Frame your photograph with red card and then stick it to the front of the card.

3 Cut the tulips from dark red card and the centre petals from medium red card and glue these in place. Trace and cut out the stem and leaves from green paper and glue these in place too, overlapping the edge of the flower.

4 Transfer two each of the insect templates but just one small ladybird to cream watercolour paper and colour with watercolour paints. When dry, use a black felt-tip pen to draw the outlines and cut out, leaving a narrow border all round. Use the picture as a guide to decorate the book with the insects, adding 'buzz' lines with the pen to create movement. Glue a wiggly eye to each bee.

Mother's Day Butterflies

Remind your mother that you are still her little girl by making this card with a picture of you both when you were younger on the front. If desired, you could add a current photograph to the back page as well.

- Card size: 45 x 8cm (18 x 3 3/16 in)
- Templates are provided on page 111

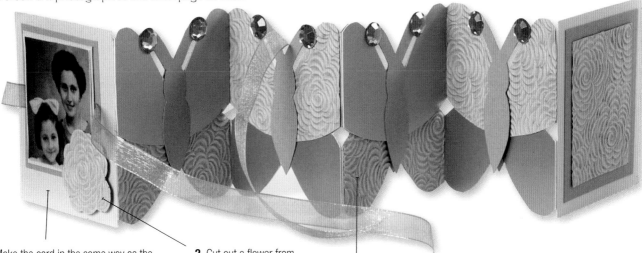

1 Make the card in the same way as the Valentine card on page 54 but using the butterfly template from page 111 and pale lilac card. Matt a photograph to lilac card and then to grey card, with a length of ribbon in between them and glue towards the top left corner of the front cover.

2 Cut out a flower from embossed paper and use sticky pads to fasten it to the bottom-right corner of the photograph.

3 Cut out two upper and two lower wings from embossed paper and shiny lilac card and four body shapes from grey card. Glue on the lower wings, alternating the embossed ones with the shiny ones and then add the upper wings. Glue the bodies over the wings and glue 1cm (3/16 in) diameter lilac coloured gems to the feelers.

Baskets of Fun

Halloween is a great occasion for everyone and it's an ideal time for making some handcrafted accessories to pump up the fun. The main event – for children at least – is collecting sweets and small Halloween toys from neighbours or at parties and other special events. These amusing card baskets are perfect for collecting or presenting the treats.

Small card baskets aren't just for Halloween – there are other occasions when you may require a container for small items, perhaps for an egg hunt at Easter or for a flower girl at a wedding. You might even want a basket to present a birthday or Mother's Day gift. You'll find further ideas to inspire you on pages 64–65.

This super pumpkin basket can be hung from its handle or displayed on a table. Line it with tissue paper and fill with sweets.

Quick and easy to make, these baskets will produce squeals of delight from excited Trick or Treaters, especially if filled with Halloween goodies. They will no doubt be treasured for weeks to come by the little ghouls, witches and zombies.

Pumpkin Basket

Made from double-sided orange and yellow card using some clever folding techniques, this pumpkin basket can be lined with tissue paper and filled with little toys or sweets as a small table gift at a Halloween party.

You will need

28cm (11in) square of double-sided orange/ yellow card

Yellow tissue paper

Basic tool kit

Basket size, including handle: 10 x 14cm (4 x 5½in)

Templates are provided on page 113

Cut two strips 1 x 21cm (⅜ x 8¼in) from adjacent sides of the square of card and put these to one side. Trace the pumpkin template from page 113 onto the yellow side of the card and cut it out. Use leftover card to cut out two eyes and a mouth.

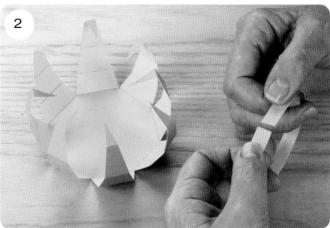

Score and fold along the broken lines to make the basket shape. Take one of the strips of card and form it into a circle, overlapping the ends by 1cm (⅜in). Glue the overlap of the strip to secure the ring.

Spacing them equally, glue the points of the basket down inside the ring, as shown. Trim the ends level with the bottom of the ring.

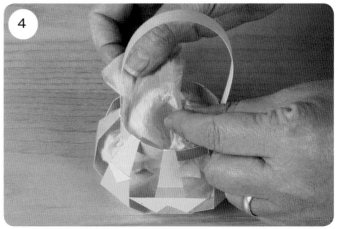

Glue the remaining strip to the inside of the circle to make the handle. Glue on the eyes and mouth. Fill the basket with scrunched yellow tissue paper.

Witch's Hat Basket

The witch's hat basket is decorated with a web cut from angel-hair paper and a bright pompom spider. Make a few to fill with Halloween treats and hang them on a bunch of twigs so that you are ready for any visiting ghouls or witches.

You will need

Black card 35 x 28cm (14 x 11in)

Cream angel-hair paper 21 x 23cm (8¼ x 9in)

Yellow card 8 x 6cm (3⅛ x 2⅜in)

1cm (⅜in) and 2.5cm (1in) diameter orange pompoms

Pair of 5mm (1/16in) diameter wiggly eyes

Basic tool kit

Basket size, including handle: 13 x 20cm (5⅛ x 8in)

Templates are provided on pages 112–113

From the black card cut two 1 x 21cm (⅜ x 8¼in) strips and two 13cm (5⅛in) diameter circles. Draw 6.5cm (2½in) diameter circles in the centre of these and cut out. Use the template to cut out the hat cone, scoring and folding along the broken lines.

Curl the cone and use double-sided tape to fasten it into shape. Cut the triangles at the top of the cone from the point to the edge. Slip the cone inside one of the circles of black card and glue in place, as shown. Trim away any excess card round the edge of the circle.

Stand the hat in a tall glass to make it easier to handle and glue the remaining black circle of card over the first circle to hide the tabs. Glue the strips of black card together and fasten inside the hat to make the handle.

Use the template on page 113 to cut out a cobweb from angel-hair paper, push it over the handle and glue it in place on the hat rim.

Cut the spider's legs from yellow card using the template on page 112. Glue the large pompom to the legs and then glue the smaller pompom on top. Stick on the eyes.

Bat Basket

The bat basket is constructed from a square of Hessian-covered card using a very simple folding technique. You can buy Hessian from specialist fabric stores or you could use a sack or a piece of coarse, undyed linen to cover your card.

You will need

Dark brown card 20cm (8in) square

Hessian fabric 20 x 30cm (8 x 11¾in)

Yellow card 5 x 3.5cm (2 x 1⅜in)

Black card 11 x 10cm (4⅜ x 4in)

Two 5mm (³⁄₁₆in) diameter brown brads

Two pairs of 8mm (⁵⁄₁₆in) diameter wiggly eyes

Basic tool kit

Basket size including handle:
10 x 15cm (4 x 6in)

Templates are provided
on page 112

Use spray adhesive to stick a 20cm (8in) square of Hessian to the dark brown card. Cut a 14mm (½in) strip from two adjacent sides of the square and divide the remainder into nine 6.2cm (2½in) squares.

On two opposite sides, cut along the drawn lines up to the intersections, as shown. Score and fold along the remaining lines.

Trim the strips of Hessian-covered card to the same length and use double-sided tape to fasten them together to make a handle. Gently ease the handle into an arched shape and use brads to fasten the ends to the sides of the basket.

On two opposite sides, push the centre square inwards and bring the outside squares around it until the points meet, as shown. Glue in place.

Fray Check

As an alternative to PVA glue, you can use an anti-fray solution such as Fray Check to seal the edges. This liquid is easily applied using the nozzle lid.

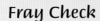

Use a needle to spread a tiny amount of PVA glue along the edges of the basket and handle to prevent fraying.

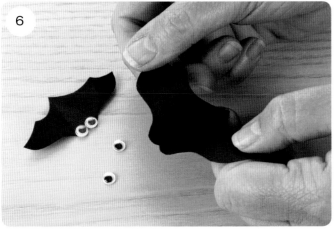

Use the templates on page 112 to cut a large and small bat from black card. Valley and mountain fold the wings and glue on the wiggly eyes. Cut a small tag from yellow card using the template and stick the small bat on top.

Glue the large bat to the handle. Fray the ends of the remaining piece of Hessian and use a few strands to tie the tag to the handle. Use the rest to line the basket.

Celebrate the difference

These small baskets are such fun that it seems a shame to limit them to one day a year, so here are a few suggestions for other adaptations. In fact, if you put your mind to it you will probably come up with a few of your own. The bat basket is especially easy to adapt – just change the colours and adornments to make one for Christmas, Fireworks Night, or even to hold birthday or Mother's Day gifts.

Chinese Lanterns

Celebrate the Chinese New Year in style with a string of decorative lanterns based on the pumpkin basket. Use double-sided card and simple embellishments to ring the changes. These lanterns could also be made for Christmas or you could use different punches and colours to create a set to hang outdoors for a summer party.

Basket size, including handle:
10 x 14cm (4 x 5½in)

Template is provided on page 113

1 Use fine gold thread to make a 7.5cm (3in) long tassel for each lantern following the instructions on page 9 and put to one side.

2 Cut out the lanterns using the pumpkin basket template on page 113 using double-sided card in your chosen colours. Use a bradawl to make a hole in the centre of each lantern base. Thread the end of a tassel through the hole from the outside to the inside of each lantern and secure on the inside with sticky tape.

3 To cover the tassel end, cut the base piece of the lantern again and glue in place, with the second colour of the card facing up. Assemble the lantern following the instructions for the pumpkin basket on page 60. Decorate with gems, gold confetti stars and punched metallic card stars.

Confetti Cone

With a simple adaptation to the brim and a radical change of styling, the witch's hat basket can be put to a totally different use – a confetti cone for a traditional wedding. You could also make a similar version for a little girl and fill it with sweets.

1 Cut the cone and handle from textured cream card – you do not need the brim. Glue the cone together then cover the triangles round the top with pale green paper and decorate each one with an iridescent flower.

● Basket size, including handle:
13 x 20cm (5⅛ x 8in)

Template is provided on page 112

2 Gather a length of 5cm (2in) wide cream lace and glue underneath the triangles round the edge of the cone.

3 Glue the handle to the inside of the cone and tie with 5mm (¼in) wide cream organdie ribbon and lace edging.

4 Glue flowers back to back in pairs with the ribbon in between near the end of each length of ribbon.

Easter Basket

The simple design of the bat basket makes it especially easy to adapt for other occasions. With just a change of colour and a few carefully chosen adornments it will be tailor-made for many different occasions. This yellow version, filled with tissue-paper strips is perfect for an Easter-egg hunt.

● Basket size including handle:
10 x 15cm (4 x 6in)

Template is provided on page 113

2 Lay the handle on your cutting board and cut three pairs of slits, one in the centre and one on each side. Thread ribbon through the slits and knot the ends together.

3 Use the template to cut two Easter eggs from green holographic card. Decorate with bows punched from gold paper. Fasten the handle and eggs to the basket with a brad through the centre of the bows.

1 Refer to the instructions on page 62 to cut the pieces for the basket and handle. Place the square on a cutting board and cut pairs of slits in the square, 5mm (³⁄₁₆in) apart, wide enough to take the width of your ribbon. Thread ribbon through the slits so that the ends are on the right side then knot the ends together. Assemble the basket following steps 2–3 for the bat basket (see pages 62–63).

Fanfare of Folds

Teabag folding, or kaleidoscope folding as it is also known, is the art of folding small squares of identically printed paper – or teabag envelopes – and combining them to create beautiful designs. You can buy special papers for teabag folding or even print free papers from the Internet and you can also use some ordinary paper or paint or stamp your own. The fabulous fans shown here were created using just one fold – the kite fold.

Once you've tried this simple technique, you'll want to continue, so on page 71 you'll find two more projects to try, this time introducing another fold, the pentagon fold. The Christmas gift box uses teabag folding in a traditional way, but the book cover combines teabag folding with some basic cutting and sticking to create an altogether different look.

Teabag papers are only 38mm (1½in) square and once folded these tiny papers look as intricate and delicate as a Fabergé egg.

These fabulous fans are made from teabag papers ➤ with a pretty Chinese-style floral design that is ideal for the motif. The purple and gold surrounds enhance the colours of the design and add a luxurious look.

Fanfare Gift Set

A fan fold is a basic origami fold, and one of the first folds that crafters new to teabag folding should learn. What better way to use this fold than to make a fan? Simply combine five fan folds and matt these together onto coloured card. Now add the tassel. Use your fan(s) on a greetings card or gift box.

For the fan card you will need

Lilac pearlescent card 21 x 20cm (8¼ x 8in)

Gold metallic card at least 14 x 20cm (5½ x 8in)

Purple card 14cm (5½in) square

Pink glitter card 4 x 20cm (1½ x 8in)

Ten 38mm (1½in) squares of floral-print teabag paper

Two small pink metallic brads

Gold embroidery cotton (floss)

Fancy-edge scissors

Basic tool kit

For the box you will need

Papier-mâché box 6 x 4 x 3cm (2⅜ x 1½ x 1⅛in)

Gold acrylic paint

Scraps of lilac pearlescent, gold metallic, purple and pink glitter card

Five quarter squares of floral-print teabag paper

Gold embroidery cotton (floss)

Pink metallic brad

Fancy-edge scissors

Basic tool kit

Card size: 10.5 x 20cm (4⅛ x 8in)

Box size: 6 x 4 x 3cm (2⅜ x 1½ x 1⅛in)

Make a tag

The small fan would make an excellent gift tag. Write your message on the back with a silver or gold pen or back the fan with pale card.

The pretty shades of pink, lilac and gold used for this card and the coordinating gift box were inspired by the colours of the teabag paper. Use the same idea to choose the card for your project.

For the fan card, start by folding the lilac pearlescent card in half widthways so it is 20cm (8in) tall. Cut a 5 x 20cm (2 x 8in) strip of gold card and trim the long edges with fancy-edge scissors. Now glue the strip of pink glitter card down the centre. Glue this strip to the card front, 1.5cm (⅝in) from the fold.

2

Fold five identical teabag squares with a kite fold, as shown below.

3

Glue the kites to a piece of gold card in a fan shape with the long edges touching. Now trim around the edge of the fan design, leaving a narrow border.

4

Glue the fan to a piece of purple card and trim around the edge again, leaving another narrow border. Pierce a hole for the brad where the points of the kite fold meet using a bradawl or pricking tool.

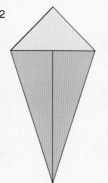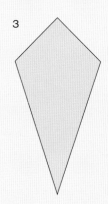

5

Make a 4cm (1½in) long tassel from gold thread (see page 9), leaving a 6.5cm (2½in) length of thread. Knot the ends and fasten the tassel to the fan by pushing the brad through the knot.

Making a Kite Fold

Fold your square in half diagonally with wrong sides together. Unfold the paper and lay it right side down on your work surface. Fold in the left and right sides so they lie along the centre line (1 and 2). Turn the paper over (3).

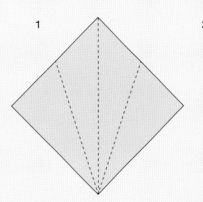

1   2   3

6

7

Cut teabag papers into quarters for the small fan. You want five identical quarters so you may be able to get four from one paper or you may need to use just one from each paper. Use the quarter papers to make a small fan in the same way as before. Add a 2.5cm (1in) long tassel. Glue the fans to the card using the picture on page 67 as a guide, holding the tassels in place with a spot of glue.

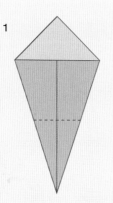

8

Make another small fan. To make a stand for the fan cut a 1.3 x 4cm (½ x 1½in) rectangle of lilac pearlescent card. Fold 7mm (¼in) towards the wrong side along both short edges. Glue one flap to the back of the fan towards the top and the other to the box.

For the gift box, paint the inside and outside of the box with gold acrylic paint and allow it to dry. Trim the long edges of a 6 x 3cm (2⅜ x 1⅜in) rectangle of gold card with fancy-edge scissors and glue to the lid with a 6 x 1cm (2⅜ x ⅜in) strip of pink glitter card down the centre. Cut a 1cm (⅜in) wide strip of lilac pearlescent card long enough to fit around the lid and trim along one of the long edges with the scissors. Glue to the lid, matching the straight edge to the top of the lid.

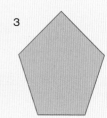

Make it again
If you have used five squares of teabag paper for the small fan, don't throw the remaining quarters away. You can make three more fans with the leftovers and use one on the gift box.

Making a Pentagon Fold

Make a kite fold as explained on page 69. Turn the folded paper back over (1). Fold the bottom point up to meet the top point (2). Turn the paper over (3).

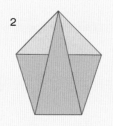

1   2   3

Celebrate the difference

Diary size: 148 x 210mm (5¾ x 8¼in)

Templates are provided on page 114

Daisy Diary

Teabag folding – and other origami folding – is perfect when you need geometrical shapes for your designs. Here, the squares are folded into pentagons to create the petals of a flower on the cover of a diary. Decorating a diary in this way personalizes it for your own use or turns a simple object into a great gift.

1 Cut three strips from striped floral paper and glue them to yellow card. Trim the strips, leaving a narrow yellow border down the long edges and glue them to the front cover of an A5 spiral-bound book. If desired, add stick-on gems to some flower centres.

2 Using the templates on page 114, cut the flower from turquoise card. Glue a 4cm (1½in) diameter circle of yellow card in the centre. Cut seven identical 2.5cm (1in) squares from the floral paper and fold with a pentagon fold (see opposite). Glue these around the flower centre. Glue the flower to the cover. Glue the stem in position underneath.

3 Kite fold a 2.5cm (1in) and a 4cm (1½in) square of striped paper for the leaves (see page 69). Glue each kite to green card and trim around the edges, leaving a narrow green border. Glue one leaf to each side of the stem.

4 Knot short lengths of ribbon and braid to the spine. As a final touch, add yellow stick-on gems to the flower centre.

Star-spangled Gift Box

This pretty Christmas box could be filled with nuts, sweets or a small gift and is suitable for any member of the family. The lid is decorated with red silver-star paper folded into kite folds and embellished with star sequins on wire stalks for added dimension.

Box size: 7.5 x 7.5 x 4cm (3 x 3 x 1½in)

Template is provided on page 114

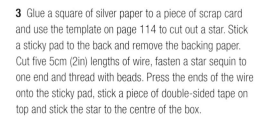

1 Cover the box with silver and red silver-star paper, following the instructions on page 11. Cut eight 2.5cm (1in) squares from the silver-star paper, fold them into kites (see page 69) and glue them to the box lid in a circular shape.

2 From the silver paper cut another eight 2.5cm (1in) squares and fold them into pentagons (see opposite). Glue these around the lid, as shown.

3 Glue a square of silver paper to a piece of scrap card and use the template on page 114 to cut out a star. Stick a sticky pad to the back and remove the backing paper. Cut five 5cm (2in) lengths of wire, fasten a star sequin to one end and thread with beads. Press the ends of the wire onto the sticky pad, stick a piece of double-sided tape on top and stick the star to the centre of the box.

In The Frame

Frames aren't just for photographs. You can frame artworks, tags, stickers or stamps – or in fact anything you want to draw attention to. And the subject doesn't have to stay inside the frame either. It can burst out or sit on top if that works better.

You can buy ready-made frames, but it's much more fun – and cheaper – to make your own. For starters, try making this 21st birthday hanging, comprising five small frames strung together with ribbon. If you don't want to hang your frames, make a standing version, like the one shown on page 78, which comes with its own decorative box, or turn your hand to some clever Christmas decorations.

These little frames were inspired by photographers' slide mounts.

This hanging says it all – there's a picture of the ➤
birthday girl, some feathers to suggest the glamour
of the day, a glass and bottle to say 'cheers' and
'21' to emphasize which birthday this is.

21ˢᵗ Birthday Hanging

A 21st birthday is such an important occasion that you'll want to make something extra special. This hanging can be folded up and placed in an envelope to make an unusual card, or you could make one to hang at a party venue or at the breakfast table.

Ready-made frames

Coloured picture mounts are available from scrapbooking suppliers. For a quick version of this hanging, use these as your frames, though note that they will be smaller than the frames used here.

These frames are decorated in a range of pinks, greys and blacks to suit the 21st birthday theme, but you could choose the recipient's favourite colours, if preferred.

You will need

- Thick white card
- Thin white card
- Scraps of black, dark green and gold glitter card
- Silver and gold metallic patterned paper 9 x 10cm (3½ x 4in)
- Paper to cover the frames (Urban Bling Paper from Me and My Big Ideas)
- Die-cut numbers
- 20cm (8in) of 5mm (³⁄₁₆in) wide gold ribbon
- 36cm (14½in) of 2.5cm (1in) wide dark pink ribbon
- 22cm (8¾in) of narrow black rickrack braid
- Small piece of pink feather trimming
- Two gold ribbon bows
- Silver key brad
- Gold cup sequins
- 5mm (³⁄₁₆in) silver gems
- Small medium and large round silver beads, oval-shaped gold plastic bugle and pink rocaille beads
- Small tassel or see page 9
- Basic tool kit

Hanging size: 63 x 9cm (25 x 3½in)

Templates are provided on page 114

Cut five 9cm (3½in) squares of thick card and use a pencil to draw diagonal lines from corner to corner on each one. Use these as a guide to draw a 5cm (2in) aperture in the centre and cut out the aperture with a craft knife and ruler on a cutting mat. Repeat to cut five frames of thin card, each with the same sized aperture.

Glue a thick card frame to the wrong side of one of the papers you are using for the covers. Trim around the edges.

Draw two diagonal lines across the paper in line with the diagonal lines on the frame. Cut along the lines and then fold back the paper flaps, as shown. Glue the flaps to the frame and trim off any excess paper level with the outside edge of the frame.

For added interest, cover two or three of the frames with two papers. To do this, glue on one paper, covering part of the frame and trim around the edges. Now glue on the other paper, overlapping the first paper slightly and again trim the edges. Cut and fold flaps of paper over to the inside of the aperture and trim off the excess as explained in step 3. Make a total of five paper-covered frames.

Decorate the frames with bows, beads, sequins, gems, ribbons and rickrack braid, using the pictures on pages 73 and 74 as your guide.

Coordination

Work on all the frames at the same time, building the decorations up bit by bit to help ensure coordination.

Fold over 7cm (2¾in) at the top of the wide pink ribbon and glue it in place. Thread the ribbon through the aperture of your first frame so that it runs behind the top of the frame and over the bottom of the frame. Glue the ribbon to the top of the frame just below the loop and to the front of the bottom of the frame. Leave the glue to dry.

Slide on the second frame in the same way and glue the top edge to the ribbon so that the second frame is 5mm (³⁄₁₆ in) below the first frame. Repeat to thread on all the frames.

Stick the thin white card frames to the back of the top four covered frames, enclosing the ribbon.

Trim the ribbon below the bottom frame, leaving about 2.5cm (1in) extending. Fold this over the back of the frame and use sticky tape to secure it in place. Now glue the thin card frame on top.

Turn the frames over carefully. Cut two 4cm (1½in) squares of gold glitter card and three 4cm (1½in) squares of black glitter card as the basis for the 'pictures'.

This frame was covered with three papers, the silver paper providing a narrow border between the animal print and the grey paper. The bottle was cut out and embellished as explained in step 13. Notice how the silver beads added to the frame suggest the champagne bubbles.

Test run

Lay out all your decorations and papers for each frame before you start sticking because it will be difficult to change things partway through.

Matt a photograph of the birthday girl onto gold card and trim around the edges, leaving a narrow gold border. Glue this to one of the 4cm (1½in) black squares and glue the square to the ribbon in the centre of the top frame. For the second frame, attach a piece of pink feather trimming to another black square with a key-shaped brad. Glue this to the ribbon in the centre of the second frame.

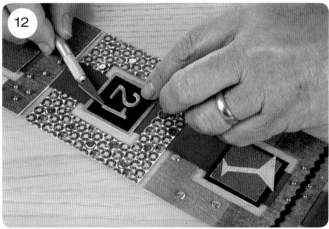

Matt the remaining black square with a smaller square of gold glitter card. Using the template from page 114, cut the glass from silver paper and glue this on top. Glue this in the third frame and add a few small silver beads for the bubbles. Matt one of the gold squares with a smaller black square and stick 21 on top. Glue this in the fourth frame.

Punch it out

Save time by using an extra-large square punch to punch the squares to go in the apertures. As long as the squares are less than 6cm (2³⁄8in) across they will fit inside the frames.

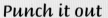

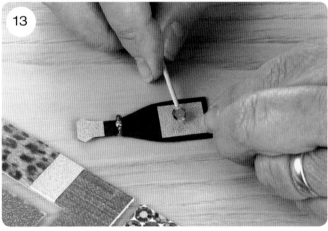

Stick a gold ribbon bow to the top of the tassel and then tape the tassel to the back of the lowest frame.

Using the templates on page 114, cut the bottle from dark green card and the bottle embellishments from silver paper. Glue a sequin to the bottle label and thread some beads round the neck. Glue this at an angle on the final gold square and glue the square into the fifth frame. If you haven't already done so, add silver beads to the frame for the bubbles.

Celebrate the difference

The idea of linking a series of frames with ribbon can be used to create booklets as well as hangings, as in the lovely christening book below, which even has a pretty matching storage box. Or if you want something completely different try the Christmas hangings opposite.

Christening Book and Box

This delightful book can be used as a shelf or table decoration in a young child's room or stored in the matching box. If you wish, you can put a photograph in each frame and keep it as a record of a young child's development.

◉ Size: 37 x 7cm (14½ x 2¾in)

1 Cut five 7cm (2¾in) square thick card frames with 4cm (1½in) apertures and cover them in patterned papers as explained on page 75. Decorate the frames with printed motifs, card, ribbon and brads. Add images behind the apertures.

2 Cut five 7cm (2¾in) squares of thin card and glue one to the back of each frame. Do not cut out the apertures as for the 21st birthday hanging.

3 Arrange the frames in order. Punch two holes on the right-hand side of the first frame, two holes on each side of the next three frames and two holes on the left-hand side of the final frame. Use ribbon to tie the frames through the holes, leaving a space between each one to allow the book to fold.

1 Cover a 9 x 9 x 6cm (3½ x 3½ x 2⅜in) square box following the instructions on page 10.

2 Cut and cover a 7cm (2¾in) thick card frame following the instructions on pages 74–75 and tie it with ribbon. Attach a photograph behind the aperture and stick it to the lid with sticky pads. Add a small tag too, if desired.

Christmas Hangings

Based on two interlocking square frames, these hangings are quick to make, which is just what you want during the busy Christmas season. The silver star hanging could also be used at a wedding or you could use balloon die-cuts for a birthday hanging.

● Silver hanging: 7.5 x 33.5cm
● (3 x 13¼in)

● Purple hanging: 7.5 x 32cm
● (3 x 12½in)

1 Cut one 7.5cm (3in) square frame with a 6cm (2⅜in) aperture from silver holographic card and another frame the same size from white glitter card. Back the silver frame with white vellum and glue a silver die-cut star in the centre. Turn the silver frame on the diagonal and push one point under the left side of the other frame; glue it in place.

3 Knot a loop in the end of a shorter length of silver thread. Decorate it with a pair of silver confetti stars glued back to back and stick it to the top of the silver frame at the back. Use this to hang your star decoration.

2 Cut an 18cm (7in) length of silver thread and glue two pairs of large silver confetti stars and one pair of die-cut silver stars together back to back with the thread in between. Make a knot in one end and stick the other end to the bottom corner of the silver frame at the back.

3 Cut another single length of red metallic thread 14cm (5½in) long and tie a loop in one end. Thread on beads again and stick the thread to the top point of the front frame at the back as a hanging loop.

1 Cut two card frames 7.5cm (3in) square and cover them with purple metallic paper. Glue gold metallic card to the back of one of them. Interlock the frames as described above. Stick a square red gem at each corner and then glue a die-cut Christmas tree to the gold metallic card and decorate with more red gems.

2 Cut a 35cm (14in) length of single-strand red metallic thread. Tie a purple tassel in the centre and thread the two ends of the metallic thread with rocailles and gold glass beads. Use sticky tape to fasten the thread to the bottom point of the front frame at the back.

Child's play

If you cut out the frames, you can then ask your children to decorate them.

Mini Memory Book

Special occasions will be remembered long after the event, and it is highly pleasurable in years to come to sit down with a book of photographs from the occasion and recall the experience. Filled with some special wedding photographs, a small album would make a wonderful thank-you gift for a bridesmaid, close family friend or anyone whose support was appreciated on the day. Use the tiny box on the front to store additional photographs or perhaps add a small item of jewellery, confetti or some other memento.

The size of this album makes it particularly attractive to children – it could be used to store special things, photographs of friends and secret notes. Instructions are given for a girl's album on page 85, and it would be a simple matter to change the colours and cover motif for a boy. Other uses for a small album like this would be to record the achievements of a child or the years of a friendship or even to showcase items you have made.

Inside there are four pages plus two pockets that can hold additional items.

The smart black and white colour combination on this album ➤ makes a nice change from the usual pastel shades associated with wedding memorabilia and it looks particularly elegant when combined with black and white photographs.

Wedding Book

This elegant album is cleverly designed with a hidden concertina spine that holds the pages and two pocket flaps for items that you don't want to stick down. The small box on the front contains a concertina-folded sheet of card to support additional photographs, enabling you to include a surprising number of images.

You will need

Two pieces of mount board 10.8 x 7.5cm (4¼ x 3in)

A4 sheet of black card

White card 30.5cm (12in) square

Daisy-patterned black-and-white paper 30.5cm (12in) square

Rose-patterned black-and-white paper 20.5cm (8in) square

Scraps of black, white and silver holographic card and black-and-white daisy and rose patterned paper

Nine 3mm (⅛in) silver brads

2m (2¼yd) of 1cm (⅜in) wide white organdie ribbon

A 3cm (1³⁄₁₆in) diameter heart punch

Empty matchbox

Silver heart-shaped confetti

Basic tool kit

Book size: 10.8 x 7.5cm (4¼ x 3in)

Cut a 13 x 7.5cm (5 x 3in) rectangle of black card and concertina fold it at 13mm (½in) intervals. Glue the two end sections to the inside of the front and back covers along the short edges.

Lay out two 10.5 x 13.5cm (4⅛ x 5¼in) rectangles of daisy-patterned paper with wrong sides facing up. Glue a rectangle of mount board in the centre of each one. Glue the edges to the mount board, first folding over the corners and gluing them down, as shown, then gluing the long edges in place.

Use black and white card and patterned paper, brads, ribbon and silver confetti hearts to decorate the pages of the matchbox and, if desired, add a few small photographs as well.

Cut two pieces of white card 15.5 x 7cm (6 x 2¾in). Using each piece, mark and score a line 5cm (2in) from one short edge and fold to make a pocket. Fasten the pocket on each side with a brad.

Cut a 50cm (20in) length of ribbon and stick it to the inside of one of the covers, 4cm (1½in) from the edge (this will be the back cover). Glue a pocket to the inside of each cover with the folded edges level with the short outside edges, as shown.

For the pages cut four 11.2 x 7cm (4⅜ x 2¾in) pieces of white card. Starting at the back of the book, attach the pages to the concertina-folded black card with double-sided tape.

Divide a 3.9 x 7.7cm (1½ x 3in) piece of black card into three 13mm (½in) sections. Score and fold along the lines and, with the book tightly closed, glue round the spine to hold the book together. Now you can decorate the pages of the album with treasured photographs.

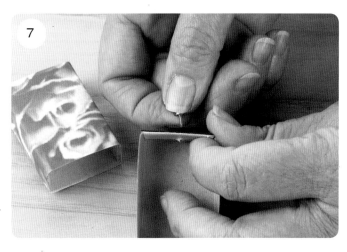

7

Pull the matchbox out of its casing. Cover the casing with rose-patterned paper then cover one short end of the box with black card. Fasten a brad in the centre of the covered end for the knob and glue a strip of white card over the brad on the inside.

8

Cut a 17 x 4.8cm (6¾ x ⅞in) strip of black card and concertina fold it at 28mm (1⅛in) intervals. Glue the bottom panel to the inside of the box.

9

Glue a strip of black card down the centre of the matchbox top, punch a heart from silver card and fasten it to the strip with sticky pads. Decorate the front of the concertina folded card with a length of ribbon and a confetti heart. Fasten the matchbox to the book by threading the ribbon through the box casing, inserting the drawer and tying the ribbon in a bow.

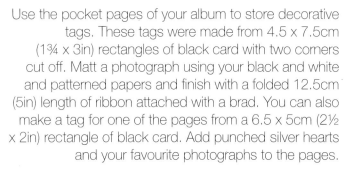

Use the pocket pages of your album to store decorative tags. These tags were made from 4.5 x 7.5cm (1¾ x 3in) rectangles of black card with two corners cut off. Matt a photograph using your black and white and patterned papers and finish with a folded 12.5cm (5in) length of ribbon attached with a brad. You can also make a tag for one of the pages from a 6.5 x 5cm (2½ x 2in) rectangle of black card. Add punched silver hearts and your favourite photographs to the pages.

Celebrate the difference

Girls' Party Book

This pretty album is designed to record a girls' sleepover party, so it only has four sides to be decorated. However, you could fit additional pages, if desired, tying them together with ribbon and eyelets, perhaps, or using staples under the spine binding.

Make the book in the recipient's favourite colours and provide embellishments for her to use on the pages.

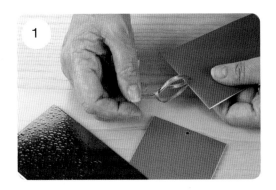

Fold the two pink rectangles in half and glue together along the short edges to make the album covers. Fold the metallic card in half in the same way to make the page. Punch a hole in the centre of the folded short edge of the pink covers. Thread each hole with a short length of lilac satin ribbon, as shown.

You will need

- Two rectangles of pink card 25 x 7.5cm (9¾ x 3in)
- Pink metallic card 23 x 7.5cm (9⅛ x 3in)
- Dark lilac card 4 x 7.5cm (1½ x 3in)
- Scraps of pink, pink metallic and dark lilac card
- Scraps of dark purple paper
- 12mm (½in) and 8mm (⁵⁄₁₆in) purple crystal brads
- Memory Mates Glamour Girl buttons
- Two 35cm (13½in) lengths of 3mm (⅛in) wide lilac satin ribbon
- Short lengths of pink and lilac ribbon and pink metallic thread
- Miniature lilac-coloured clothes pegs
- Basic tool kit

- Book size: 12.5 x 7.5cm (5 x 3in)
- Template is provided on page 114

Place the pink metallic page between the two covers with the folds facing the same way and use double-sided tape to stick the pages together at the unfolded ends. Make the spine of the book from the dark lilac card, folded in half and glued to the covers.

Use the template on 114 to cut out three pink metallic and two dark lilac panels for the fan. Use a bradawl to make a hole in each panel and join them together with a large crystal brad. Glue the fan to the front cover. Use the remaining materials to decorate the pages of the book.

Pricked to Perfection

From the 18th century right through to Victorian times, paper pricking was used to create pictures and cards. Costumed figures, lace borders, monograms and verses were pricked with a pin or spiked wheel and sometimes coloured. Here the technique is combined with watercolour to create crocus and daffodil designs on an Easter card and gift bag.

For some simpler alternatives you'll find three colourful Christmas baubles on page 93, which are made using metallic paper and trimmed with sequins, beads and sparkling ribbon for extra shimmer. Alternatively, try the innovative scented sachets on page 92. Fill them with crushed pot pourri or spices for Christmas or prick a floral design and fill with lavender to make a scented drawer sachet.

Pricking is used as a drawing tool to mark outlines and add detailing to the fresh daffodil motif on this pretty card.

Nothing says 'spring' more than daffodils and crocuses, which is why these lovely bulbs feature on this card and matching gift bag. They are ideal for an Easter or Mother's Day present or you could use the same idea with other motifs and colour combinations to suit any season or celebration.

Daffodil Card

Usually pricked designs are worked on white or off-white paper to emulate fine lacework but this card brings in another paper-craft technique – watercolour. The two techniques work really well together to create the unusual design on this card.

You will need

- **Yellow card 19 x 14cm (7½ x 5½in) and 5.7 x 12.7cm (2¼ x 5in)**
- **Dark green paper 11 x 12cm (4⅜ x 4¾in) and 6.3 x 13.5cm (2⅜ x 5¼in)**
- **Cream watercolour paper 13 x 14cm (5 x 5½in)**
- **Watercolour paints in yellow and green**
- **Basic tool kit**

Card size: 14 x 13cm (5½ x 5in)

Template is provided on page 115

The soft colours on this daffodil are achieved using several thin washes of colour, building up the tones gradually. Alternatively, you could use inks to give a vibrant effect or diluted acrylics.

Fold and score the 19 x 14cm (7½ x 5½in) rectangle of yellow card 6.5cm (2½in) from the left-hand short side. Matt the flap with the 6.3 x 13.5cm (2⅜ x 5¼in) rectangle of green paper, aligning it with the centre edge. Then matt the remaining piece of yellow card on top of this, again aligning the centre edge, as shown here.

Trace the daffodil from page 115 and use low-tack tape to fasten it over the rectangle of cream watercolour paper.

3

Lay the watercolour paper and tracing on a pricking mat (or see the tip, right). Hold the pricking tool vertically and prick out the design with evenly spaced holes – imagine your pricking tool is a sewing-machine needle.

Practice makes perfect

Although pricking is easy, don't expect to get it right first time. Practice on a scrap of your chosen paper before you begin so you can gauge the depth necessary to make the correct hole size.

Make your own

If you don't have a pricking mat and pricking tool, use a piece of polystyrene or dense foam to prick on and push a needle into a cork to make your pricking tool.

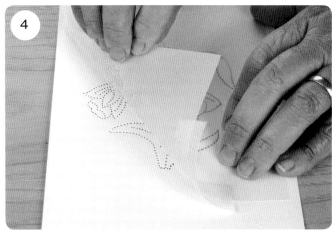

4

Once you've pricked along all the lines, remove the tape from one edge of the tracing and flip the tracing back to reveal the pricked design. Check that you haven't left any gaps or missed any sections of the design before removing the tracing completely.

5

Now use yellow and green watercolours to paint the daffodil design. Take your time with this stage and aim to use several tones by diluting your watercolours to different degrees. Leave the paint to dry.

6

Glue the design centrally onto the 11 x 12cm (4⅜ x 4¾in) rectangle of green paper with the bottom of the stalk level with the lower edge. Now draw a line at the top of the green paper 5.5cm (2³⁄₁₆in) from the left side. Cut along this line and round the right side of the daffodil, leaving a narrow green border. Matt the design to the card flap, aligning the straight edge at the top with the front of the card.

Daffodil Gift Bag

This little gift bag is made from a pale green paper with a yellow card border around the top to provide strength for the handles. It features the same pricked and painted daffodil motif as the card and a coordinating crocus tag. It's perfect for a small gift such as a scarf or perfume – or perhaps for a little book or album that you've made yourself.

You will need

Pale green paper 39.5 x 33cm (15½ x 13in)

Dark green paper 10.5 x 12.5cm (4⅛ x 5in), 12 x 14cm (4¾ x 5½in) and 5 x 10.5cm (2 x 4⅛in)

Yellow card 39.5 x 6cm (15½ x 2⅜in), 11.5 x 13.5cm (4½ x 5⅜in) and 6.5 x 10.5cm (2½ x 4⅛in)

Cream watercolour paper 20 x 14cm (7¾ x 5½in)

Two 18cm (7in) lengths of green cord

Basic tool kit

Bag size: 12.8 x 6.4 x 27cm (5 x 2½ x 10½in)

Templates are provided on pages 115 and 119

Following the measurements in the diagram on page 119, draw the template for the bag onto the pale green paper. Cut out, score and fold along the dotted lines. Use the pattern for the top strip to cut out a 39.5 x 6cm (15½ x 2½in) piece of yellow card. Score and fold it in half along the long centre line and then along the other lines. Lay the main part of the bag on your work surface and stick the strip of yellow card to the underside of the top edge using double-sided tape. Repeat with the front edge of the paper.

Glue the sides of the bag together and fold and stick the bottom flaps. Leave the glue to dry.

3

Prick the daffodil design onto cream watercolour paper and paint it with watercolours in the same way as for the card (see page 89). Cut out the daffodil, leaving a narrow border, and glue it to the 10.5 x 12.5cm (4⅛ x 5in) rectangle of dark green paper.

4

Now matt the daffodil to the 11.5 x 13.5cm (4½ x 5⅜in) yellow card and then to the 12 x 14cm (4¾ x 5½in) piece of dark green paper. Glue the whole lot to the front of the bag, just above the bottom edge.

Adding a message

Write on the tag before you attach it to the handles – it's much easier that way.

5

Repeat step 3 using the crocus design on page 115 but don't matt it onto paper. Stick the small green rectangle onto the small yellow rectangle and trim off the top corners to make a tag. Stick the crocus in place and then punch a hole in the top centre of the tag.

6

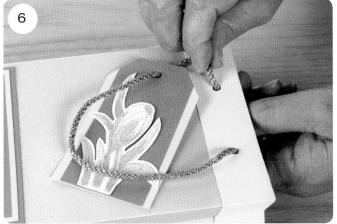

Nip the bag together at the top along the scored lines and punch a pair of holes in the yellow card. Pass a length of cord through the holes on the back of the bag to make a handle and then knot the ends. Repeat on the front of the bag, this time adding the tag.

This pretty crocus motif is ideal for a tag and gives the gift bag added colour. The tag itself is easy to make by matting one strip of card onto another and then trimming the top corners to create the shape.

Celebrate the difference

Here are two more novel ways of using pricking. The pricked holes allow scents to permeate through, so pricking works wonderfully for making paper sachets that you can fill with pot pourri or lavender and pop in a drawer. Similarly, pricking the Christmas Baubles allows light to shine through the holes to create a stunning effect against the eyecatching metallic card.

Scented Sachets

Drawer sachets are usually made from fabric and you might wonder how paper could work. The answer lies in the hidden muslin sachet that holds the filling and the holes in the paper that let the scents permeate out. Filled with crushed pot pourri or spices, these sachets make the perfect gift.

- Holly sachet: 14 x 11cm (5½ x 4½in)
- Snowflake sachet: 11.5 x 11.5cm (4½ x 4½in)
- Templates are provided on page 116

1 Using the template on page 116, prick the snowflake design onto a 12.5cm (5in) square of medium blue pastel paper. Cut out the design, leaving a narrow border.

2 Paint the oval shapes and the area in between the lines with silver acrylic paint and use silver glitter glue to make dots around the border and snowflake, finishing with a large dot in the centre.

3 Make a bag from muslin to fit inside the centre rectangle, fill with crushed pot pourri and tape to the back of the pricked paper. Stick 6mm (³⁄₁₆in) wide double-sided tape to the wrong side between the straight lines and stick the design to a slightly bigger piece of silver metallic card. Trim the edge, leaving a narrow border.

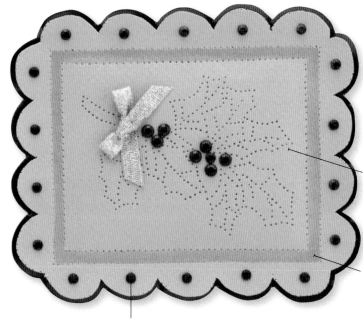

1 Using the template on page 116, prick the holly design onto a 12.5 x 15cm (5 x 6in) rectangle of medium green pastel paper. Cut out the design along the outside line.

2 Paint the area in between the straight lines with gold acrylic paint. Make a bag from muslin to fit inside the centre rectangle, as snowflake sachet above.

3 Decorate the sachet with red gems for berries and a gold ribbon bow.

Christmas Baubles

Take some brightly coloured metallic card, prick on a simple design, add embellishments and hang up to make an eye-catching window decoration this Christmas. It's easy to do and no one else will have such stylish and unusual decorations.

- Bell: 8 x 9cm (3⅛ x 3½in)
- Fat bauble: 7.5 x 7.5cm (3 x 3in)
- Teardrop bauble: 6 x 9cm (2⅜ x 3½in)
- Templates are provided on page 116

Work in layers

You can actually prick through two or three layers of paper at once, so if you want several baubles in the same design, though not necessarily in the same colour, stack two or three sheets of paper and then prick out the design through all layers at once.

1 Trace the bell pattern from page 116 and prick the design onto turquoise metallic card. Cut out, leaving a narrow border, and punch a hole at the top.

2 Use the picture as a guide to glue the gold sequins in place and then prick a circle of holes around each sequin.

3 Add a gold bow just below the hole. Finally, use a length of gold thread to hang the bauble.

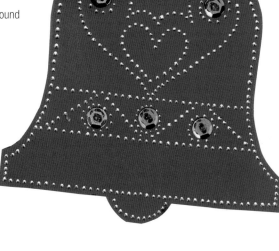

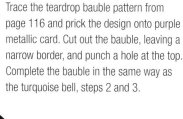

Trace the teardrop bauble pattern from page 116 and prick the design onto purple metallic card. Cut out the bauble, leaving a narrow border, and punch a hole at the top. Complete the bauble in the same way as the turquoise bell, steps 2 and 3.

Trace the fat bauble pattern from page 116 and prick the design onto pink metallic card. Cut out the bauble, leaving a narrow border, and punch a hole at the top. Complete the bauble in the same way as the turquoise bell, steps 2 and 3.

Cut-out Cards

It seems that everyone is making their own cards these days, and you need something unusual to keep ahead of the game. Shaped cards are always interesting without being too complicated or time-consuming to make, and these are the sorts of cards that it's useful to make a stock of so you can always have one when it's needed.

The handbag card shown opposite is an excellent and versatile design that could be adapted in many ways with different colours and embellishments to create special looks for special friends. You'll also find a fan, cake and gift shape on pages 98–99 to further your options.

Fancy brads add to the three-dimensional element of this card and provide classic styling.

This particularly elegant card would be ideal if you are ▸ giving vouchers or money for a birthday or for many other occasions). Its colours emulate those of an expensive leather bag, but of course you can use whatever colours you think would suit the recipient.

Handbag Birthday Card

This unusual card is lots of fun but really elegant at the same time, making it useful for many occasions. It would be great for someone who is going away or who has just started his or her first job, or it could be useful for Mother's Day or a birthday. Then again, you may just want to make it and keep it.

You will need

- A4 sheets (US letter) of pale green card
- A4 sheets (US letter) of heavyweight double-sided gold metallic paper
- Two 1cm (⅜in) orange crystal brads
- Two 5mm (³⁄₁₆in) orange crystal brads
- 2cm (¾in) diameter bronze coloured brad
- 4mm (³⁄₁₆in) hole punch
- Velcro dot
- Basic tool kit

- Size excluding handle: 15 x 10cm (6 x 4in)
- Templates provided on pages 117 and 119

Check before sticking

Before you glue the shapes onto the handbag in step 2, cut out the flap lining and lay it in position at the top edge of the bag. That way you can be sure that none of the shapes will be hidden under the flap later.

Use the pattern on page 119 to cut the handbag from green card. Score and fold along the fold lines.

From the metallic paper cut four shapes using template 1 and two using template 2 (see page 117). Punch 14 circles. Turn the handbag over and glue two of shape 1 and eight circles to the front of the handbag, as shown.

Turn the card so that the flap is at the bottom and insert the bronze-coloured brad 3cm (1¼in) from the bottom edge. Cut the flap lining from gold metallic paper and glue it to the inside of the flap. (It is larger than the flap, so make sure it is centred.)

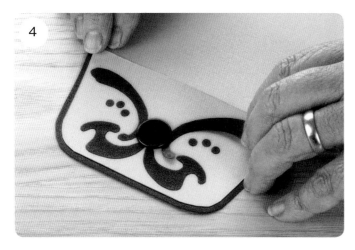

Glue the remaining paper shapes to the front of the flap, tucking them under the bronze brad.

Remove the attachments from the back of the orange crystal brads using a small pair of pliers. Use glue dots to fasten a large orange brad to the bronze coloured brad, with a small one on each side.

To make the handle, cut an 18 x 2cm (7 x ¾in) strip of metallic paper and fold it diagonally so that the ends will fit in the slits.

Push the ends of the handle through the slits at the top of the bag and glue them to the inside of the flap. Fasten a large orange crystal brad to a 2.5 x 1.5cm (1 x ⅝in) piece of green card and fasten to the centre of the handle (see the photograph on page 94). To fasten the bag, stick a small Velcro dot under the flap.

Ribbon strap

Instead of cutting card for the handbag strap, use an 18cm (7in) length of 2cm (¾in) wide grosgrain ribbon. This will add further texture and will fold easily into the envelope.

Celebrate the difference

There are plenty of motifs that make good cards. The trick is to look for simple shapes with no small details extending that could easily get bent or crushed in transit. The cake and gift shapes shown here are good examples of suitable shapes.

Mother's Day Fan

This unusual card is designed for Mother's Day, but it would be equally popular as a birthday card for a young girl. Once you've cut out all the pieces it is quick to assemble and to decorate using punched bows and stick-on gems.

● Card size: 18 x 10cm (7 x 4in)
●
● Templates are provided on page 118

1 Use the templates on page 118 to cut seven fan struts from turquoise glitter card and seven bases from silver metallic card. Glue a base in position on each strut and use a bradawl to make a hole in each strut base. Punch seven bows from silver metallic card and glue one to each fan strut.

2 Insert a 1cm (⅜in) diameter crystal brad through the holes in all the strut bases to fasten the fan together.

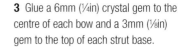

3 Glue a 6mm (¼in) crystal gem to the centre of each bow and a 3mm (⅛in) gem to the top of each strut base.

4 Punch two more bows and glue them together back to back. Glue a large crystal gem in the centre. Attach the bow to a silver tassel and tie to the brad at the base of the fan.

Wedding Cake

This card would make an excellent wedding invitation or a thank-you card for someone who has really helped at the wedding, such as the matron of honour, mother of the bride or even the florist. It's quick and easy to make using white card and peel-offs.

- Card size: 11.5 x 19.6cm (4½ x 7¾in)
- Templates are provided on page 118

2 Glue the middle and top tiers in place, each one overlapping the lower tier slightly. Define the front edge of each tier with a double row of peel-off strips.

3 Stick three silver butterfly peel-offs to white card and fill the body and part of the wings with waste peel-off pieces. Punch two hearts from white marbled paper and glue these together. Crease the butterfly wings and glue one to the hearts and the other two to the 'top' of the middle and bottom tiers. Add iridescent fabric flowers and small flowers punched from marbled white paper, with a bead or gem in the centre. Glue the hearts to the top of the cake and add a scattering of sequins.

1 Cut the three cake tiers from white card using the templates on page 118 and fold the bottom tier in half.

Wedding Present

A gift motif is so versatile that you'll probably find yourself adapting this card for other occasions. The lilac card features a white glitter-card bow, which is fixed to the card with sticky foam pads to enhance the three-dimensional effect. Peel-off bows add decoration in an instant.

- Card size: 12 x 12cm (4¾ x 4¾in)
- Templates are provided on page 117

1 Use the template on page 117 to cut the card blank from lilac card and score and fold along the dotted lines. From white glitter card, cut a strip 1 x 16.5cm (⅜ x 6½in) and the three parts of the bow.

2 Glue the strip to the centre of the flap and the front of the card, with a peel-off strip on each side. Make the bow by fastening the three pieces together with foam pads and glue over the strip at the top of the card. Stick peel-off bows to pale lilac metallic paper and infill some areas with waste peel-off. Cut out carefully and glue to the card.

Templates

Here are the templates that you will need to complete the projects in this book. Most are full size, but if any enlargement is necessary a note beside the template will tell you how much to enlarge by.

Key

Cut along these lines ——————

Score and then fold --------- along these lines

Making Templates

Refer to the following instructions to trace and use the templates.

Lay tracing paper over your chosen template and go over the lines with a sharp HB pencil.

Turn the tracing over and lay it on a piece of white paper. Rub along all the lines with your pencil. Turn the tracing over again and place it on a sheet of thin white card. Draw over the lines again with the pencil. Mark the front of the template and cut out.

Chapter one

Cut each piece once unless otherwise stated

Baby Girl Pocket Book

Tag

Christmas Tree Decoration

Christmas tree

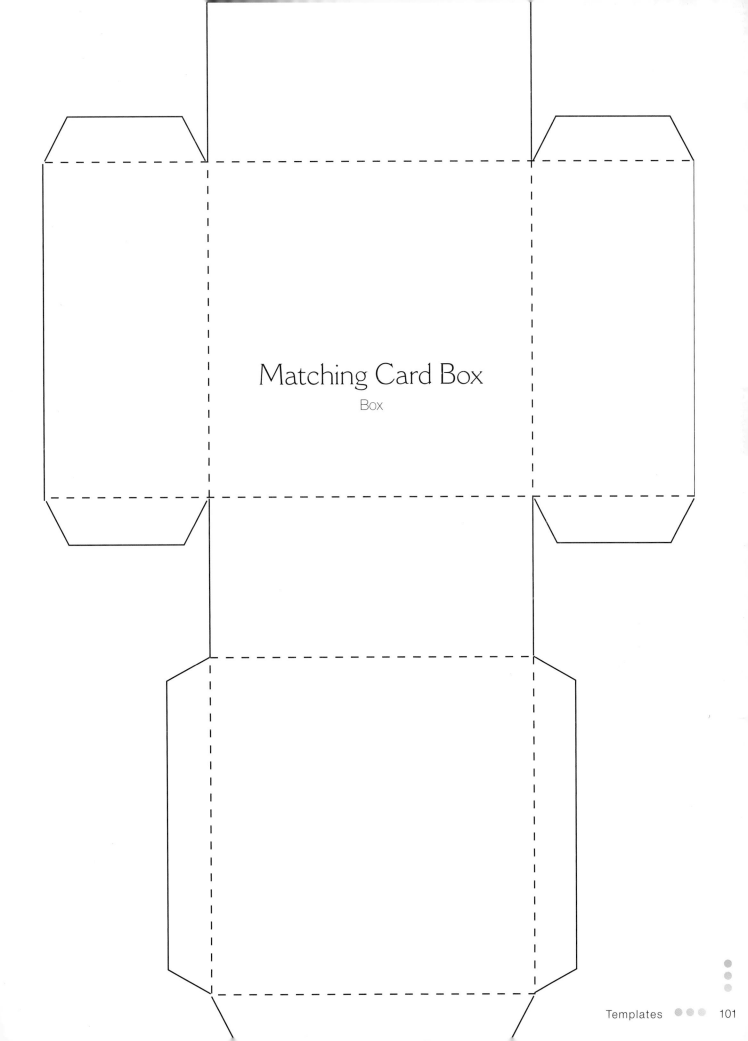

Matching Card Box

Box

Chapter two

New Home

Cat

Chimney

Window, cut 2

Window box, cut 2

Grass, cut 2

Table rim

Table

Centre medallion

Table base

Door

Door panelling

Sky

House

Path

House and Garden

Grass

Nativity Card

Mary, Jesus and crib

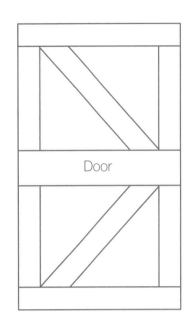

Door

Crib base

Tree trunk

Left-hand panel

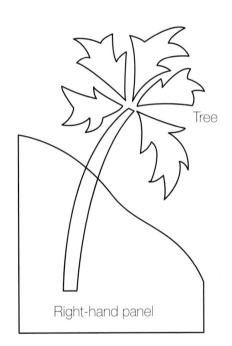

Tree

Right-hand panel

In His Shed

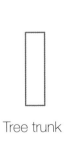

Tree trunk

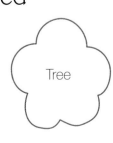

Tree

Workbench

Chapter Three

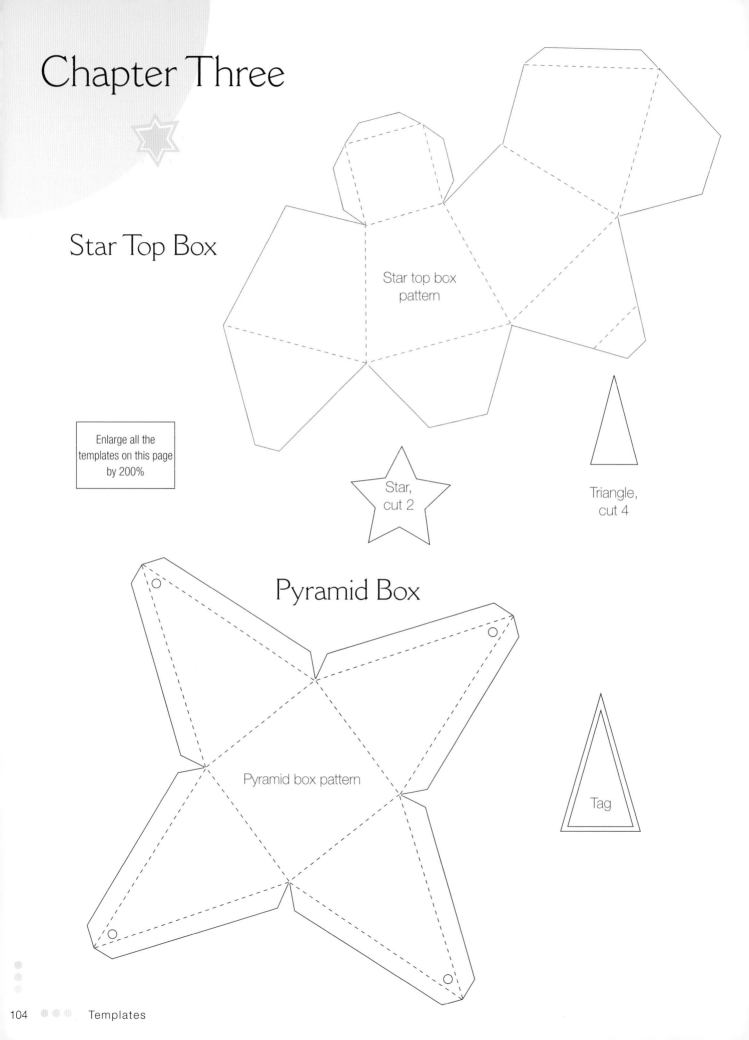

Star Top Box

Star top box pattern

Enlarge all the templates on this page by 200%

Star, cut 2

Triangle, cut 4

Pyramid Box

Pyramid box pattern

Tag

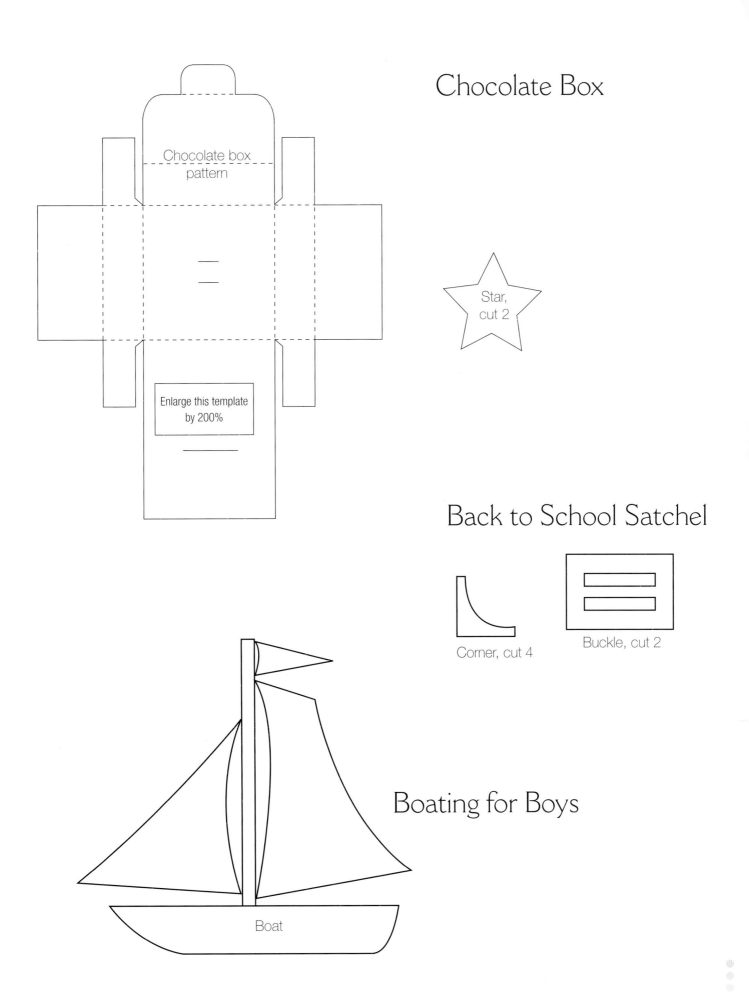

Chocolate Box

Chocolate box
pattern

Enlarge this template
by 200%

Star,
cut 2

Back to School Satchel

Corner, cut 4

Buckle, cut 2

Boating for Boys

Boat

Chapter four

Baby Memory Box

Teddy

Silver Wedding Album

Champagne glass

Teddy tag

Car tag

Men's Gift Bag

Car

Chapter five

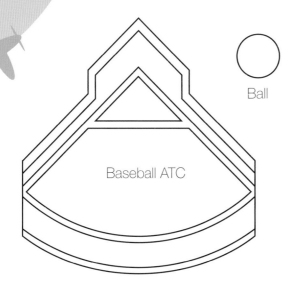

Baseball ATC

Ball

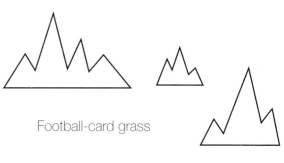

Football-card grass

Rugby-card grass

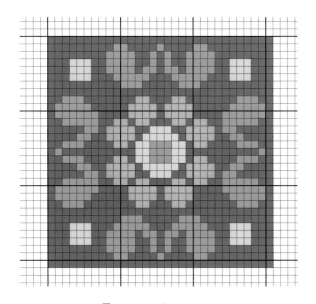

Tapestry chart

Mother's Day Hobby Set

Dressmaker's dummy

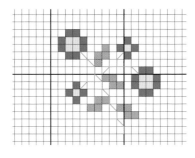

Cross-stitch chart

Chapter six

Front cover

Heart frame

Wings, cut a
symmetrical pair

Valentine Card

Heart card template
9 x 11.3cm
(3½ x 4½in)

Photo pockets

Keyhole pocket

Key

Wrapped
heart

Heart frame

Arrow pocket

Arrow

Envelope heart

Small heart

Heart envelope

Blue for a Boy

Teddy

Shorts

Nappy

Romper suit

Shoe

Braces

Waistcoat

Tulip Birthday Card

Tulip

Flower, cut 4

Insects

Centre petal, cut 4

Leaves and stem, cut 4

Mother's Day Butterfly

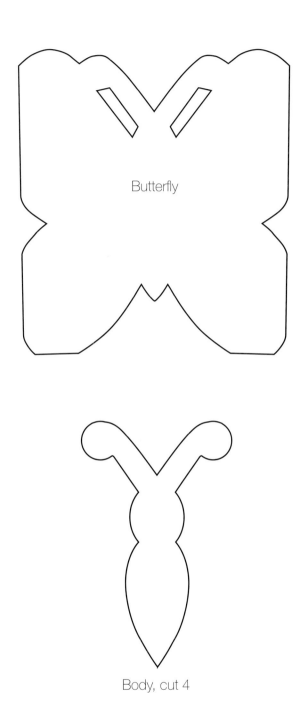

Butterfly

Body, cut 4

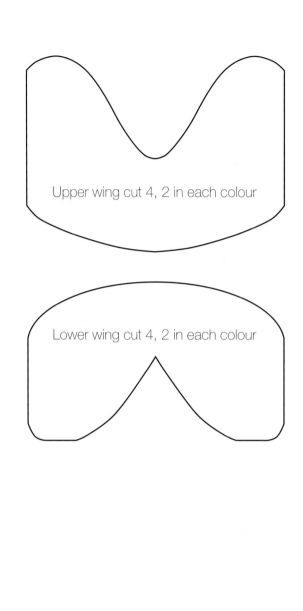

Upper wing cut 4, 2 in each colour

Lower wing cut 4, 2 in each colour

Chapter seven

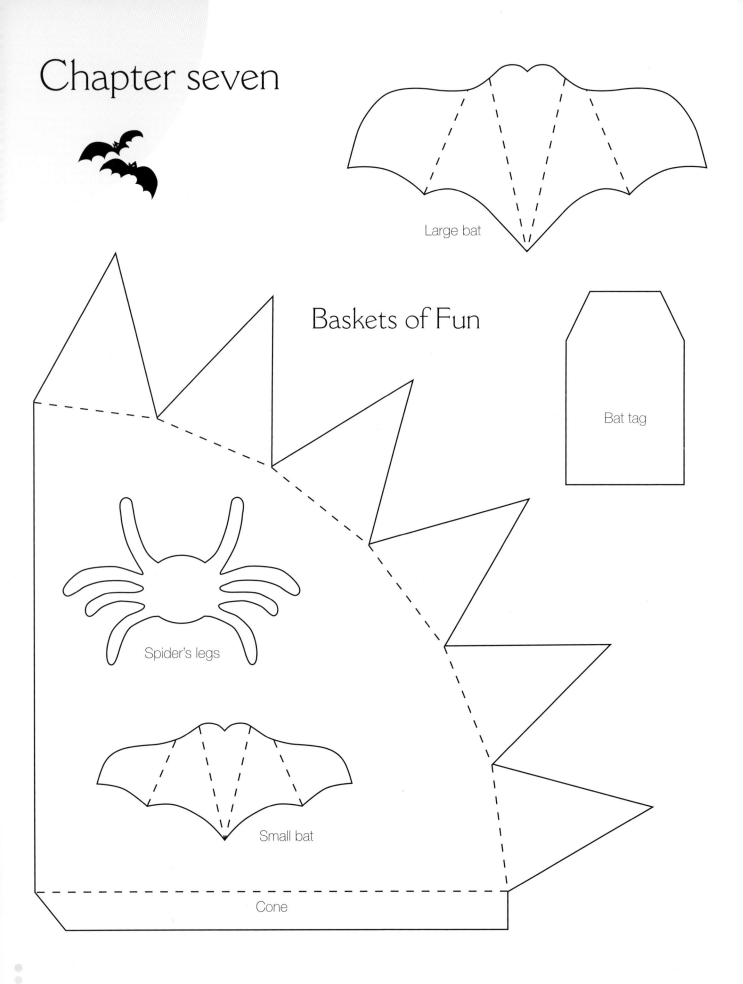

Large bat

Baskets of Fun

Bat tag

Spider's legs

Small bat

Cone

Witch's Hat

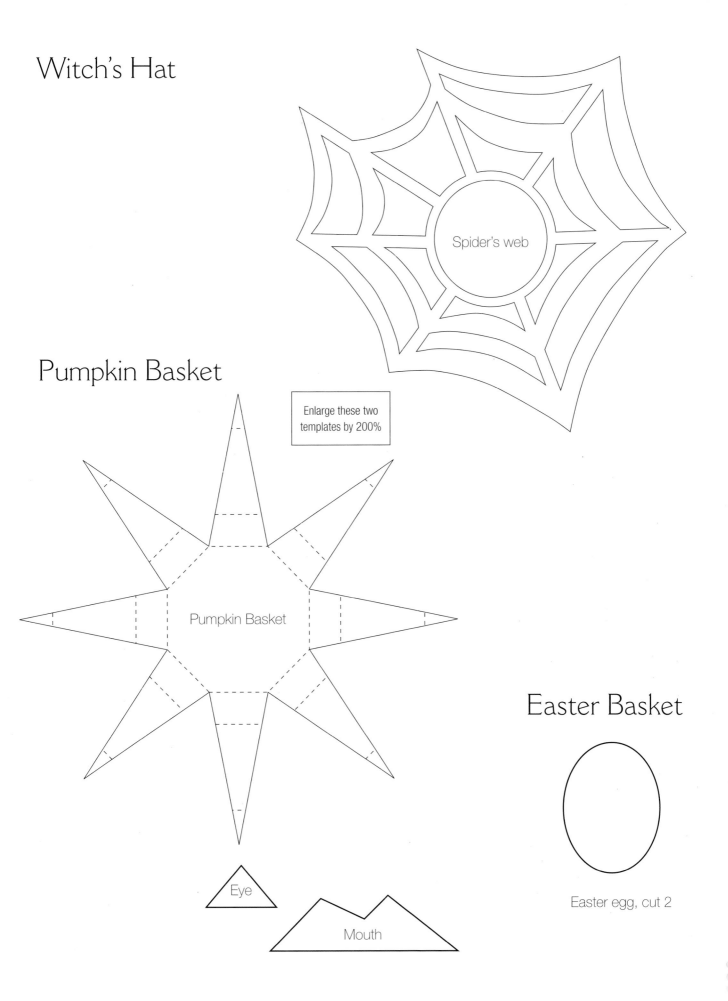

Spider's web

Pumpkin Basket

Enlarge these two templates by 200%

Pumpkin Basket

Eye

Mouth

Easter Basket

Easter egg, cut 2

Chapter eight

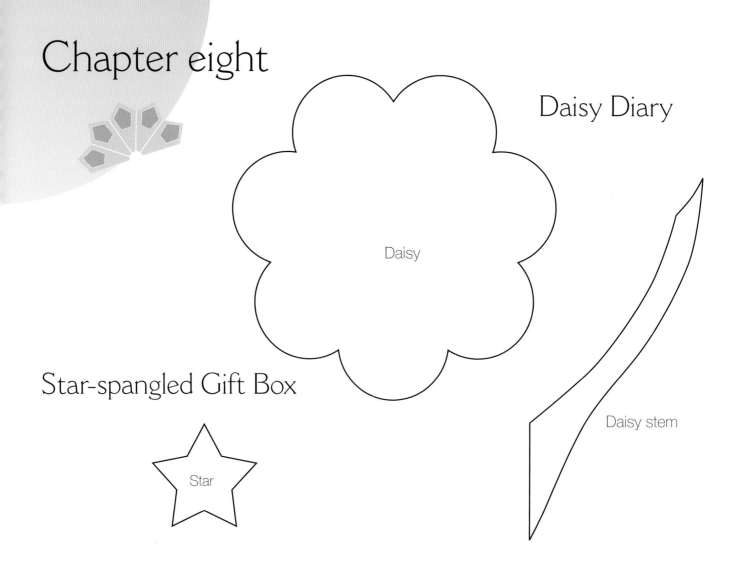

Daisy Diary

Daisy

Daisy stem

Star-spangled Gift Box

Star

Chapter nine

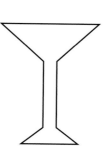

21st Birthday Hanging

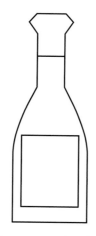

Champagne bottle

Champagne glass

Chapter ten

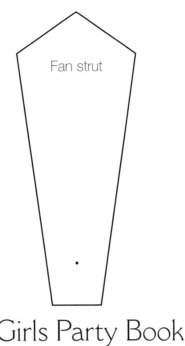

Fan strut

Girls Party Book

Chapter eleven

Daffodil Card

Crocus

Daffodil

Scented Sachets

Christmas Baubles

Snowflake sachet

Holly sachet

Bell

Fat bauble

Teardrop bauble

Chapter Twelve

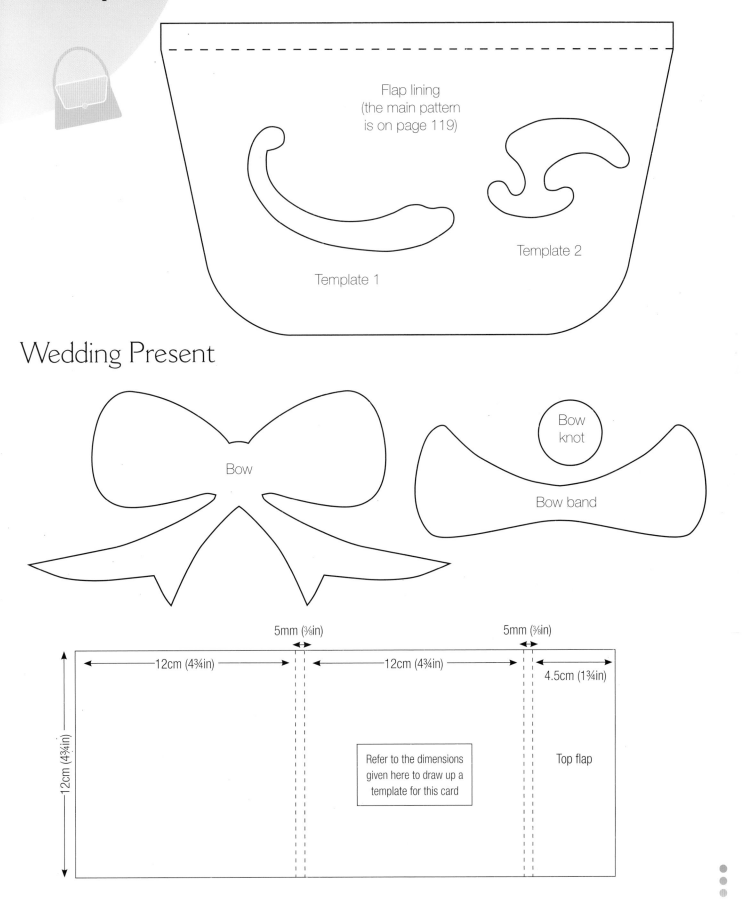

Flap lining
(the main pattern
is on page 119)

Template 1

Template 2

Wedding Present

Bow

Bow knot

Bow band

5mm (³⁄₁₆in)

5mm (³⁄₁₆in)

12cm (4¾in)

12cm (4¾in)

4.5cm (1¾in)

12cm (4¾in)

Refer to the dimensions
given here to draw up a
template for this card

Top flap

Mother's Day Fan

Fan strut, cut 7

Base, cut 7

Top tier

Bottom tier

Wedding Cake

Middle tier

Handbag Birthday Card

Handbag (flap lining
is on page 117)

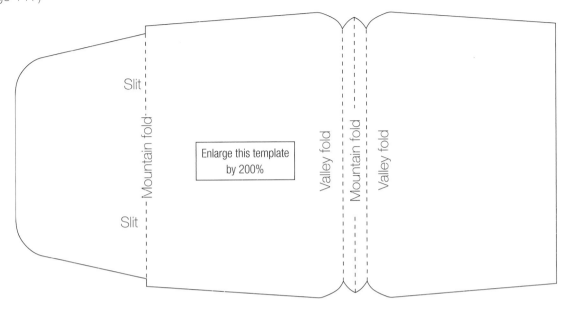

Slit

Mountain fold

Slit

Enlarge this template
by 200%

Valley fold

Mountain fold

Valley fold

Daffodil Gift Bag

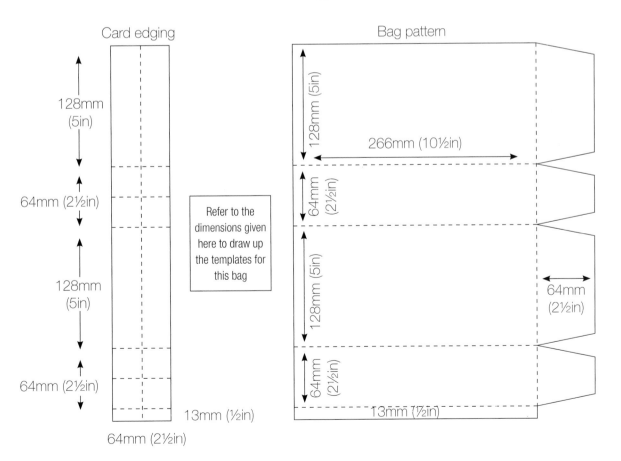

Card edging

128mm
(5in)

64mm (2½in)

128mm
(5in)

64mm (2½in)

64mm (2½in)

Refer to the
dimensions given
here to draw up
the templates for
this bag

Bag pattern

128mm (5in)

266mm (10½in)

64mm
(2½in)

128mm (5in)

64mm
(2½in)

64mm
(2½in)

13mm (½in)

13mm (½in)

Suppliers

UK

Button It
23 Hannah Way
Gordleton Industrial Park
Pennington
Lymington
Hampshire
SO41 8JD
Tel: 01590 681611
e-mail: button-it@customlaser.co.uk

CDS Superstores/The Range
York Road
Doncaster
DN5 8 LY
Tel: 01302 787070
e-mail: doncaster@therange.co.uk

The Craft Room
4 Alexander Walk
Lincoln
LN2 4FN
Tel: 01522 537389
e-mail: caroline@thecraftroomuk.co.uk

Craftime Ltd
Unit B2 Willow Way
Sherwood Business Park
Annesley
Nottinghamshire
NG15 0DP
Tel: 01623 722828
e-mail: sales@craftime.co.uk

Crafty Individuals
Tel: 01642 789955
e-mail: crafty.individuals@ntlworld.com

No.9 Paws for Thought
9 Steep Hill
Lincoln
LN2 1LT
Tel: 01522 510524

Trimcraft
Mancor House
Bolsover Street
Hucknall
Nottingham
NG15 7TZ
Tel: 0115 9834805
e-mail: kerry@midgrp.co.uk

US

Fascinating Folds
PO Box 10070
Glendale AZ 85318
www.fascinating-folds.com
An extensive supplier of reference
materials for paper craft.

**Hollanders Decorative and
Handmade Papers**
410 N Fourth Avenue
Ann Arbor NI 48104
Tel: 734 741 7531
www.hollanders.com
Supplier of unique decorative papers
plus stationery.

Paperarts
www.paperarts.com (Arizona)
Wide range of exciting papers.

Papermojo
papermojo.com
Tel: 1 800 420 3818

Twinrocker Handmade Paper
100 East 3rd Street
Brookston
IN 47923
www.twinrocker.com
Supplier of handmade paper and
importer of decorative papers.

About the Author

Jane Alford has had a very successful career as a needlecraft designer and author, running cross stitch businesses for many years before reinventing herself as a craft, card making and papercraft designer. She currently works as a freelance designer for various craft magazines and since 2005 has been a demonstrator for Trimcraft. Jane lives in Lincoln, UK.
email: janealforddes@hotmail.com

Acknowledgments

As well as thanking family and friends for their support, I would also like to thank the following:

Cheryl, Beth, Charly, Eleanor and Betsy at David and Charles. They have allowed me freedom to interpret my ideas and for that, I thank them.

To Karl Adamson, whose patience and professionalism produced such great photographs.

Kerry at Trimcraft, Liza at Craftime and Karen at The Craft Room, for generously providing many of the materials used in this book

Index